Acclaim for *I Get It!*

"I Get It! is an insightful roadmap and coaching tool for young high potentials. It's also a great reference for experienced managers looking for an edge."

—**PETER JACKSON**, VP Finance, Lennox International

"I've been striving for years to explain 'it' to those who 'don't get it.' This book is spot-on for coaches, mentors or developers of talent. This will become my most recommended must-read!"

—**MARTY PHILP**, former President, Ingersoll Rand Security & Safety, Canada

"Simplify and succeed! A great primer for any up-and-comer...as well as a refresher for seasoned managers."

—**TOM MAGULSKI**, CEO, Dover Partners

"I tend to gloss over books focused on the latest business fad of the day. This one is different: readable...practical...with immediate application."

—**RICK KILEY**, CEO, gThankYou!

"I Get It! shows people how to wake up to the reality of business."

—**STEPHEN SHERWOOD**, author, *Finding Freedom*

"This is one of those rare books that combines proven business practice with practical guidelines for operators in the real world."

—**DAVID WOODS**, President and CEO, AIA Corporation

"Finally, a solution for what's been driving me mad for decades! Witmer has helped to open a dialog with my people that will help them exceed my expectations."

—**KEVIN CHOKSI**, CEO, Workforce Software

"In the sea of management books only a few stand out. I Get It! should be on your nightstand."

—**TOM QUINN**, President, Kirtland Community College

"This explains why I often feel alone running my business."

—**KENT MISEMER**, President & CEO, Liberty Propane

"A great tool to help executives understand the power of simplicity...at all levels of the organization."

—**GARY KUBERA**, President & CEO, Canexus Limited

"It amazes me the number of leaders who just 'don't get it.' The opportunity that confronts these leaders is of immense importance to the success of the business. I have spent many years in HR in Europe and the US and have seen the same issue on both sides of the pond."

—**JIMMY JOHNSTON**, Senior VP HR, GKN Aerospace PSSP

"Clear, concise management fundamentals you must know and practice for successful execution."

—**RICK SCOREY**, President & CEO, Freedom Technologies

"Neil Witmer's *I Get It!* is essential reading for those aspiring to break out of middle management and into 'big' leadership roles. It will help you leverage your personal brand, deliver results and understand the stakeholders who will drive your success."

—**MIKE HARRIS**, Former CEO, Paradigm Precision Holdings

"Witmer offers a comprehensive map to help the reader simplify essential relationships with colleagues and team."

—**ED CATENACCI**, Director HR, Coty Inc.

"Dr. Witmer 'gets it', illustrated by his simplified, concise collection of the fundamentals. Why didn't someone outline these basics to me years ago?...I could have avoided a lot of painful potholes."

—**CHUCK TURNBULL**, Private Equity CEO

"In my fifteen years of working with Neil, I've always been impressed with his ability to cut through the noise and get right to the heart of the matter. He has done so again with *I Get It!*—great real-world advice for real-world success."

—**JIM BREWER**, VP Operations, Encompass Lighting Group

"Getting it is one of the best ways you can advance your career in any complex organization. Nothing is more frustrating to a leader than dealing with an employee that just doesn't get it."

—**CHRISTINE GOODSON**, Director Global Talent Sourcing, SPX Corporation

"Life is too short to be confused in today's complex business world. Neil's clear, focused guidance is a terrific roadmap for making sure you and your team 'get it.'"

—**TOM RIORDAN**, President and COO, Terex Corporation

"With *I Get It!,* Neil Witmer demonstrates not only that he's got it...but that he can communicate what it is and how others can get it too."

—**STEVE THOMPSON**, Principal, Sterling Partners

"...insight in an incredibly simple format, Witmer nails down one of the great executive development dilemmas..."

—**ALAN TRAYLOR**, VP International Operations, Dycor Global Solutions

"Neil strips away fads and focuses on the key fundamentals of management! This book will be required reading for my team."

—**DANIEL SHANE**, VP Integration and European Services, SPX Flow Technology

"*I Get It!* is a great collection of experiences and a quick reference for managers. Readers learn how to simplify complex issues and how organizations build culture."

—**VAUGHN SIMON**, President (retired), Hartco Flooring Company

"*I Get It!* identifies the critical ingredients that distinguish successful leaders. People at any level can apply these principles and be assured that their value and performance will increase. Dr. Witmer's perspective on leadership is profound in its clarity of message and specific in its call to action for those who want to improve both individual and organizational success. Everyone should have a copy on their desk."

—**DEWAYNE PINKSTAFF**, President and CEO, Metokote Corporation

"Witmer captures a deep practice map for management skill, business street smarts and effective leadership."

—**JOHN MCGINNIS**, Private Equity CEO

"The fundamentals that Neil Witmer brings forward in *I Get It!* are of great value for improved collaborative success."

—**DENNIS FEDOSA**, CEO, Agricredit Acceptance

"A highly versatile PhD who—get's it! *I Get It!* is wisdom that is so simple if you read it and get it—the world can become your oyster. A must-read for all learning organizations."

—**JIM PERRY**, Global VP HR, Master Chemical Corporation

"*I Get It!* nails the fundamentals of high-performance leadership. Neil Witmer has captured what it has taken me a career to fully understand and appreciate, and that should be a real career boost to those who take it to heart."

—**DOUG RAHRIG**, Director Global Materials R&D, Brady Corporation

"Witmer's stories and examples illustrate straightforward, simple fundamentals and serve as a guidebook for executives—or for those who aspire to be. I can hardly wait for this book to be published. I have a number of CEOs and executives that I must give it to—and then use the exercises for coaching."

—**GIL HERMAN**, Group Chair, Vistage International

"I wish I had this book earlier in my career. I had to learn to 'get it' the hard way."

—**JIM CATES**, General Manager, ATK Integrated Weapon Systems

"Witmer has written a primer for effectiveness at any level within an organization. Anyone who wants to play on the A-team should read this book."

—**STEWART CRAMER**, CEO, LAI International

"An indictment of complication—A celebration of common sense."

—**ROGER BYFORD**, CEO, Vocollect

"Get it, got it. Neil Witmer puts the sense back in sensibility."

—**GREG JEHLIK**, CEO

I Get It!

Simplified Fundamentals
Your Manager Badly Wants You to Know
… and Do

Neil Witmer, PhD

This edition published by
Dog Ear Publishing
4010 W. 86th Street, Ste H
Indianapolis, IN 46268

www.dogearpublishing.net

ISBN: 978-160844-224-9
This book is printed on acid-free paper.

Printed in the United States of America

Contents

Acknowledgments   ix

1   **INTRODUCTION**   1

2   INWARD   **Be Real**   9

Admit What Your Colleagues Already Know about You   10
Take a Hard Look at Your Core Values   11
Balance Ego and Modesty   14
Put Your Stake in the Ground, Firmly   18
Develop Your Signature Style   19

3   UPWARD   **Exceed Expectations**   23

Understand Your Manager's Core Values   23
What if Your Boss is the CEO?   27
Learn to Fly at 30,000 Feet, Even if You're Not a Frequent
Flyer   29
Articulate Defensible Points of View   32
Stay Focused in the Face of Being Overwhelmed   34
Avoid Surprises at All Costs   38

4   DOWNWARD   **Create Accountability**   41

Upgrade Talent as if Your Career Depended on It   41
Clarify and Align Priorities   46
Reduce Uncertainty   51
Delegate "Unreasonably"   54
Obsess over Metrics   57

5   SIDEWARD   **Influence Others**   61

Understand the Real Motives of Your Colleagues   62
Listen 'til It Stops Hurting   65
Elevate Self-Esteem   67
Develop Trusting Relationships   70

Contents

Generate Controversy to Gain Respect   74

6   OUTWARD   **Develop Business Acumen**   79

Get Strategy   80
Embrace Customer and Shareholder Reality   82
Become Financially Astute   84

Appendix—Versatility Worksheet   93
Notes   95
Index   99

Acknowledgments

Thanks to Jeff Grip, my business partner of many years, who has broadened my thinking and greatly improved the clarity of my writing. My partner and mentor Steve Sherwood has helped challenge beliefs and assumptions, leading to many of the core concepts in this book. Steve Yastrow and Caroline Ceisel provided advice on branding, focusing on the point of view of the reader. Stephanie Seifert, my copy editor, helped remind me that I didn't major in English. Countless colleagues and clients provided material and stories. Specific thanks go to Stewart Cramer of LAI, Rick Abraham and Chris Croner of SalesDrive, Joe Wright and Jim Perry of Master Chemical, Bob Spath, Jim Babiasz of Fisher & Company, Mike Harris, Jim Cates and Dan Olson of ATK Integrated Weapon Systems, Carl Willis of ATK Armament Systems, Drew Ladau and Ann Cope-Place of SPX Thermal Product Solutions, Mort Mortenson of M. A. Mortenson Company, John Altstadt of Gibraltar Industries, Lee Johnson of Navistar, Phil Sauder, and Dave Dailey.

There is no adequate way to acknowledge the support given by my family, Mary Pat, Paige, and Hallie, who have long tolerated my passion for my work and my love affair with my laptop.

Chapter 1

INTRODUCTION

"He gets it!"

—A delighted CEO

The phrase *"get it"* makes immediate sense to business leaders, like a knowing grunt between old friends. Those who *get it* are business-savvy, focused, and like-minded. Those who don't *get it* are technically narrow or get caught up in non-value–added pursuits. *Getting it* does not automatically come with tenure. Even senior management can fail to *get it*.

A few years ago, I consulted with a private equity firm, helping it assess candidates for key positions. Its boards often lamented underperforming CEOs who didn't *get it*. So we interviewed a number of board members. We also interviewed the CEOs themselves. Not surprisingly, we found that CEOs believed that their boards didn't *get it*, either. The term *get it* was a gut-level punch, immediately riveting the attention of all parties. We used this emotional energy to create a communication tool, the *Get-It Profile*, to help each side align its expectations of the other.

Getting it applies equally to all levels, from the corner office to the janitor's closet. There will always be people who understand business fundamentals. And there always seem to be people who don't.

Warning Signs That You Are Not *Getting It*

- Senior leaders become impatient with you or ignore you altogether.
- You don't always get private jokes at work.
- You run out of conversation topics with fast-track peers.

Getting it has nuances in diverse industries—government contracting, growth businesses, turnarounds, or fast-changing technology firms. One could define unique *get-it* formulas for each these industries; however, it is more interesting to look at similarities across industries. In most organizations, *getting it* refers to the management and leadership behaviors that create results and define a positive culture. Not unlike the extraordinary formulas described by Jim Collins in *Good to Great*[1], there are best practices in management that are universally effective.

More specifically, when we listen closely to the frustration and excitement of top leaders in our multi-industry client base, the same themes emerge again and again. These leaders are desperate to find managers who can

- **Simplify** what is overly complex.

- Focus on **fundamentals** rather than faddish trends.

- Apply this wisdom in **all directions**: inward, upward, downward, sideward and outward.

Let's look more closely at what it means to *get* these three themes.

Simplify

The term "simple" has a long history. Early Romans used *simplus* in much the way we use the concept. Copernicus achieved notoriety with a simpler theory of the solar system.[2] Occam's razor[3] (not the shaving kind) argued that the simplest explanation tends to be the best. Genghis Khan achieved victory with simplified battle strategies.[4] Henry David Thoreau, when asked the secret of life, replied, *"Simplify, simplify, simplify."*

Today, managers are increasingly compelled by simplicity because their lives have become so overwhelming and complex. Searching with the words "simple" and "management" together produce more than 100 million Google hits. Every experienced manager has stories about the frustrations of complication. Unnecessary theory...bureaucratic policy...overanalysis...lack of common sense. Not *getting it*.

Why does complication remain such a chronic problem in business? To make this discussion easier, let's disregard those forces that cannot be controlled by an organization, such as government regulation, global competition, and resource scarcity. Aside from these forces, most complexities are very much under an organization's control.

To understand people's tendency to complicate, let's first look to psychology. It is human nature for people to habitually do what they most value. Oddly enough, people complicate their lives because they value complication. Yes, even you and me. Different types of managers value different types of complication:

- Bright, conceptual managers get bored once they become competent at their jobs. To stimulate their minds, they create complexity. Mental exercise. Self-indulgence, actually.

- Competitive managers try to show each other up during meetings. Each person adds a better idea to the mix.

- Insecure managers are afraid to speak up when they encounter illogic or see colleagues getting caught up in personal agendas. They value others' approval over defending their own beliefs.

Because most management teams have their fair share of bright, competitive (and sometimes insecure) people, the inevitable result is complication.

"You have a compelling idea when you can condense it to three bullets and explain it in 10 seconds."

—An executive who *gets it*

Complication can cause a leadership team to go for months, even years, with burdensome strategies or overcommitted initiatives. In the worst case, a powerful leader who loves complexity will create a bureaucratic culture that breeds inefficiency, rule-bound thinking, and other forms of nonsense. Sometimes even the CEO doesn't *get it*.

Obviously, complexity is not always bad. Complexity is often required to create value. Look at recent innovations in software, automotive safety, pharmaceutics, and energy production. New technologies are exponentially more complex than in the past, and more valuable. Similarly in business, success formulas have become more complex in the disciplines of strategy, marketing, supply-chain management, product development, and ERP systems. Thriving in business today, and anticipating tomorrow's changes, requires the ability to think, plan and act in multiple dimensions. Further, it can be argued that future technology and social policy relating to economic

3

prosperity, healthcare, energy, and national security must necessarily become more complex to keep pace with an increasingly complex world.

It is precisely because of this inevitable trend that managers must not add unnecessary complexity to the mix. In other words, savvy managers must embrace necessary complexity with an eye toward keeping things as simple as possible. They go about their increasingly subtle work with a bias toward simplicity.

Avoiding Naïveté

> *One day, people saw teacher Nasruddin out in the street searching frantically for something. "What are you searching for?" They inquired.*
>
> *"I've lost my key," replied the teacher. So everyone joined him, trying to help him.*
>
> *After much searching, someone had the urge to ask the place where, exactly, the key was lost, so that a more focused search could be made.*
>
> *"I lost the key in the house," he replied matter-of-factly. "Then why are you searching for it in the street?" was the obvious question asked of him.*
>
> *"Because there is more light here"!*

"Simple" can be derogative, describing someone who is "common, ignorant or mentally deficient." Naïve. Foolish. Naiveté leads to costly error. This is not a formula for effectiveness.

> *"Everything should be made as simple as possible, but not simpler."*
>
> —Albert Einstein

So how do you, the savvy manager, *get* simplicity and avoid being simplistic or naïve?

One way is through experience. Effective performers are typically weathered by multiple job rotations, educated in the ways of the world, and often scarred by hard lessons. Eyes wide open. Shrewd. Over time, they learn to avoid pitfalls, potholes, and people who manipulate. But this does not mean that they are intellectually complicated. The most successful executives learn to think and act both shrewdly *and* simply.

Another solution is to learn from experienced people—mentors, teachers, role models—or from authors who bring you the benefit of their unique experiences. In this vein, *I Get It!* aims to provide shortcuts for you if you either lack experience or are looking for proven formulas.

Sometimes mentors and authors provide lessons that are not apparent on the surface. Alan Greenspan, Chairman of the Federal Reserve for 18 years, was widely recognized as extraordinarily successful. Oddly, his complex verbiage became his trademark. For example, he said: "Being able to rely on markets to do the heavy lifting of adjustment is an exceptionally valuable policy asset. The impressive performance of the U.S. economy over the past couple of decades, despite shocks that in the past would have surely produced marked economic disruption, offers the clearest evidence of the benefits of increased market flexibility."[5]

The principles Greenspan used to guide policy, however, were often simple.[6] His language stemmed partly from his wry sense of humor, intentionally teasing those who dissected and overinterpreted his meanings. Picture him, with huge glasses and sly grin, saying, "I've been able to string more words into fewer ideas than anybody I know."

Getting it, then, is to strive for simplicity without being naïve, to be shrewd without complication. And, hopefully, having a touch of humor.

Fundamentals

"Fundamental," meaning "original, essential, of central importance," traces its roots to the 15th century. In music, a fundamental is the note that gives a chord its basic harmony. The opposite of fundamental is "secondary, superfluous." In business, lack of attention to fundamentals is common:

- Fixing symptoms rather than root causes

- Designing initiatives based on the latest book the CEO is circulating

- Being politically safe rather than challenging sacred cows

- Continuing to pursue failed methods while hoping for a different result

Not surprisingly, human nature is often to blame for ignoring fundamentals, just as it is responsible for complication. Bright, competitive (and sometimes insecure) managers often pursue personal agendas rather than proven principles. Or they lack experience and try to reinvent the wheel.

Fundamentals are not hard to identify or learn. If you look at successful management practices, you will see that most can be reduced to fundamentals. For example, LEAN manufacturing is based on the core principles of improved efficiency, cost, and quality.[7] These same principles underlie other process-improvement technologies—six sigma, reengineering, kanban, JIT, TQM, policy deployment, kaizen, quality circles. Unfortunately, each successive evolution of terminology seems to be driven more by entrepreneurial authors than breakthrough innovation. Cleverness sells more books than standardization does.

A similar pattern occurs in approaches to leadership—theory Y, theory Z, situational leadership, employee involvement, the "way of the aardvark." Although these methods address a wide range of goals, many share a common set of principles. Their popularity is more a function of the marketing budgets of consulting firms than of profoundly new ideas.

I do not mean to be too critical, however. Fads can have value. Why not create productive change by capturing your people's imaginations with compelling "new" ideas? Recent innovations in product quality and productivity improvement would not have occurred without the aura of innovative programs.

Buzzwords are often short-term, however, satisfying the need for an eager program sponsor to pursue the latest and greatest or for a CEO to sponsor innovation, not because of strategic necessity but from a personal need to self-stimulate. The program sustains only as long as upper management shows interest. Recently, our consulting firm conducted in-depth interviews of 35 CEOs, attempting to understand the driving values behind their habits and whims. The #1 conclusion—83% of the CEOs were driven by a need to stimulate their extraordinarily ambitious and conceptual minds (more in Chapter 3). Although their intentions are typically honorable, CEO judgment is always colored by personal values, sometimes practical…sometimes not.

Managers who *get it* have learned from, and survived, these fads. They tend to revert to proven approaches, relying more on fundamental principles and plain language than the flavor-of-the-day. And if something new comes along, they adapt it in a practical way, taking advantage of the energy the new "buzz-fad" creates.

Let's look at this from one more angle. "Fundamental" can also mean "belonging to one's innate characteristics," as in "Cindy has a fundamental talent for coaching." Early in career, it is difficult for any manager to truly know and use a natural style. Most novice managers wing it, perhaps guided by Management 101 training. They are hungry to copy techniques to help them be more effective. They often fixate on successful leaders in the organization, puzzling over how those leaders are so effective. Over time, novice managers stop copying others and discover methods that come naturally to them. Hopefully, what comes naturally is also fundamental. Sadly, some mid-career managers are still searching for their own fundamental ways. More on this in Chapter 2.

Pragmatism, Not Fundamentalism

History tells of zealots—people who latch onto a rigid belief system to satisfy a deep need for security and the satisfaction of self-righteousness. Today, fundamentalism is alive and well in politics, religion, and business. Like most -isms, fundamentalism restricts clear thinking and free choice. It is more concerned with conforming to a strict set of beliefs than following a pragmatic result.

Fundamentalists focus on *what's right*, whereas managers who respect fundamental principles focus on *what works*. To see the value of fundamental business principles, managers must freely question their own ideas—and the ideas of others.

This Book

The following pages outline 24 simplified, proven fundamentals that are typically mastered by managers who *get it*. Although some management books aim to be comprehensive, such as Heller and Hindle's 861-page *Essential Manager's Handbook,*[8] our aim is to be sufficient. These fundamentals were chosen because they are the formulas that early-career managers seek and seasoned managers wish their people would *get*. The goal, other than keeping this book short, is to define the practices that underlie successful performance of the best managers we have seen in the field. There is little theory here but lots of practicality. The chapters of this book are organized in five areas:

Chapter 2 (INWARD) aims to give you, whether you are novice or seasoned, the guidance to be authentic, transparent, and compelling toward others. By first knowing your innate strengths and shortcomings and then unleashing your natural, signature style, you will operate with greater confidence and decisiveness. Anyone who is *real* is more likely to *get it*.

Chapter 3 (UPWARD) provides insight into the mindset and passions of upper management. One goal is to help you exceed the expectations of challenging bosses. Another goal is to help you figure out if top management, or a CEO's job, is a desirable place for you to aspire.

Chapter 4 (DOWNWARD) covers five key fundamentals of creating a high-performing and accountable staff. The themes are well known, focused on talent, priorities, delegation, and metrics. Rather than rehashing theory, our purpose is to summarize practical techniques.

Chapter 5 (SIDEWARD) outlines techniques for interpersonal influence, perhaps one of the most challenging skill sets for any manager or leader. Although this chapter could easily expand into a book itself, following the few simple formulas provided will give you a distinct advantage over less-skilled colleagues who *don't get it*.

Chapter 6 (OUTWARD) helps you look beyond yourself and colleagues to the broader context of business. This includes a focus on customers, shareholders, strategy, and financial metrics.

Where Do *You* Stand?

After you explore the following chapters, you may wish to evaluate your own *get it* skills. To help you do this, we offer tools and consulting assistance. Please go to http://www.WitmerAssociates.com for information.

Chapter 2

Be Real

"You can't understand business until you understand people, and you can't understand people until you understand yourself."

—Michael Bayles, former Group President, Quanex

Your manager secretly wants you to be "real." Yourself. Transparent. Not strained or posturing. Your CEO is always watching from the corner office for ANYONE who shows signs of being open, self-assured, purposeful, and authentic. Hopefully, it's you. Hopefully, you *get it*.

Being real means standing out from the crowd in a natural way. Speaking up decisively. Maybe doing it differently. Certainly, doing it *your* way. Some managers are naturally real. They understand their strengths and shortcomings and aren't afraid to disclose them. They are modest without compromising their confidence. They make decisions quickly without self-doubt or second-guessing. They aren't afraid to be themselves.

Warning Signs of Not Being Real

- You feel the need to conform to others' expectations.
- You hesitate to admit your shortcomings publicly.
- You don't yet believe that you've earned the right to propose a radical idea.

Some managers are not real. They can be duplicitous or political. They try too hard to meet others' expectations. They are often tense and wary, hoping that colleagues won't see their flaws. They get suckered into ego games or defensiveness. They convey insincerity and thus are hard to trust.

Fortunately, there are simplified fundamentals that anyone can follow to be more real. The first one requires you to be completely open and self-disclosing, to yourself and others.

Admit What Your Colleagues Already Know about You

> *"Tell people the truth, because they know the truth anyway."*

> —Jack Welch, former Chairman, GE

Everyone has shortcomings, often justifying or denying them. You may have a touch of arrogance that you see as confidence. You may silently judge the people around you, feeling smugly proud of your shrewdness. You may not admit that your boss intimidates you (but of course he really IS intimidating). You may not know how to fix a performance problem in your staff and don't want to admit it. To *get it*, you must first show your colleagues that you *get yourself*.

Our 360° survey research over 15 years, dissecting the skills of thousands of managers, shows that 88% of managers possess at least one career-limiting skill gap. Seventy-three percent possess at least two. More surprisingly, 92% of managers are blind to at least one aspect of their performance.

You may suffer the illusion that your flaws are well hidden or that your opinions are evident only when spoken. Even if you are the kind of person who readily admits that you have shortcomings, you may not come completely clean with others, or yourself. You are more transparent than you think. And your colleagues are more insightful than you think. Research on nonverbal language shows that only 7% of the impact of a person's message comes from his or her chosen words, while 93% comes from tone of voice and nonverbal behavior.[1] We might as well be living in glass houses.

Our colleagues or spouses often have realistic views of how we behave and why. When my wife hung a framed aphorism beside my bathroom sink—"Feelings are Everywhere, Be Gentle"— was I surprised at her hint? Yes, actually. Although I know that I can be critical and outspoken, my Achilles' heel is understanding the emotional impact of my behavior. My wife has secretly wished for years that I *get* her feelings. Although I still suffer from this flaw, at least now I readily admit it.

There is an old saying, "*Understanding* the problem is the booby prize." Of course the real goal is to *fix* it. Still, merely admitting the truth about a flaw starts to degrade its power over you. If you admit a truth to yourself, it becomes perhaps 20% less powerful. If you then disclose it to others, it loses perhaps another 20% of its power. Over time, the more you publicly tell the truth about yourself, the more power you have and the more respect you earn. As such, self-disclosure is key to self-understanding. It also shows others that you *get it*.

> *"Ye shall know the truth, and the truth shall set you free."*
>
> —Jesus

> *"There are only two mistakes one can make along the road to truth: not going all the way, and not starting."*
>
> —Buddha

> *"If you tell the truth, you don't have to remember anything."*
>
> —Mark Twain

Take a Hard Look at Your Core Values

In Chapter 1, we observed that people's values can cause them to complicate business, losing sight of common sense. Your core values will always color your operating style, sometimes in a productive way, and sometimes not.

For example, why do many managers work hard to improve their time-management skills but continue to firefight? Or learn assertiveness techniques but still avoid conflict? Or vow to eat healthy food but still binge on Häagen-Dazs®?

It boils down to core values. For instance, if you value spontaneity more than self-discipline, you will remain disorganized. If you value others' approval more than getting results, you will avoid conflict. If you value short-term pleasure more than avoiding the risk of heart

11

disease, you will eat fried foods and ice cream. Based on 15 years of coaching high-potential managers in our *Unleashing the Leader Within*™ program, we have learned several things: One, even high performers are haunted by less-than-productive values. Two, values don't change easily, but you can *amplify* productive values which can then overshadow the unproductive ones. Three, awareness and acceptance of one's core values is the first step to developing a real, high-performing style.[2]

How do you identify your core values? Not by listing your philosophies and beliefs. Your beliefs may reflect your values, but they don't dictate which values influence your behavior. These three predictors are more dependable indicators of true values:

1. your habits

2. your emotional flares

3. where you invest your time and money

"What a person is, is what a person does."

—Ernest Hemingway

Take a few minutes to make some notes in the worksheet on the following page.

Interpreting our behavior is advanced stuff for most of us. It takes diligence, patience, self-honesty, and, often, a professional coach or counselor. For example, what is the meaning of "I have a habit of procrastinating expense reports until the last minute"? Does this mean that you are lazy? Or lack prioritization skills? Maybe you value variety over routine or are uber-strategic and not interested in detail.

Taking this further, what if you procrastinate on all projects until the last minute, even the interesting ones? Does this mean that you like to flirt with danger? Don't have enough drama in your life? Or do you secretly want to tweak your boss's nose because you have an authority problem?

Another example: A common experience of talented managers is feeling impatient when listening to slow or overly detailed people. If you are impatient with others, does it mean that you are results-oriented? Are intolerant? Have attention-deficit disorder? Psychology is often complex and elusive, but it is important for you to become psychologically minded to develop advanced skills.

Worksheet to Brainstorm Your Core Values

List examples of your *habitual behavior*, those things that you do repeatedly and consistently at work. This includes tasks that are most enjoyable to you and those things that you have a reputation for doing.	Stemming from the patterns of behavior in the left column, what appear to be your underlying values?
Make a list of any *emotional reactions* you have felt, or shown, in the past year at work. These could be positive emotions or negative emotions (joy, excitement, frustration, anger, apprehension).	
List how you spend most of your *time* and *money* at work.	

Steve Sherwood, author of *Finding Freedom: The Five Choices that Will Change* Your Life,[3] has devoted his career to helping people understand and change their behavior, both professional and personal. He uses a technique to help people deeply examine their personal values, something he calls *hunting yourself down*. With this process, many people understand, sometimes for the first time in their lives, why they do what they do.

Other authors, such as Eckert Tolle in *The Power of Now,*[4] take the art of self-awareness to a spiritual level. Many people use their spirituality as a powerful catalyst to crystallize a personal vision or a clearer sense of purpose in their work. Whereas bible thumpers tend to promote someone else's doctrine, spiritual managers tend to operate from a personal, natural set of beliefs. They probe thoughtfully and deeply into their values and behaviors.

By understanding the values behind your behaviors, you will do more than just develop self-awareness. You will feel more comfortable in your own skin, using your natural skills. You will more easily articulate your operating style and development needs to others, including your manager and others who are concerned with your development. Understanding your core values is not a quick task you can check off your list; it requires ongoing dedication. But it is worth the effort, and is prerequisite to *getting it*.

Balance Ego and Modesty

People who *get it* are skilled at balancing two very different aspects of their personalities—ego and modesty. They do this naturally, without effort. They are real in the way they behave.

There is a common misperception that ego is bad and modesty is good. When most people say that someone has an ego, they are usually referring to self-centered arrogance. Modesty is commonly seen as lack of ego, i.e., humility or consideration. There is a more useful way to look at this, however.

In business, ego can be defined as "sense of self"; thus, if you have a strong ego, you are confident, ambitious, outspoken, and willing to take risks. Ego strength is required for performance and image as a leader. Ego, then, is not arrogance. Similarly, low ego is not modesty. Low ego reflects followership traits such as self-consciousness, caution, and compliance. Imagine a scale of Ego Strength, from high to low:

High	Ego Strength	Low
Confidence		Self-Consciousness
Willingness to Risk		Cautiousness
Outspokenness		Shyness
Imposing One's Will		Bending to Another's Will
Leadership		Followership

Note that neither arrogance nor modesty is on this scale. These traits can be drawn on a separate dimension, as illustrated below. Modesty is the stuff of service, empowerment, trust, and other powerful leadership traits. Low modesty indicates arrogance and a host of unproductive traits.

High	Modesty	Low
Listening		Arrogance
Other-Centeredness, Giving		Self-Centeredness, Dominating
Service to Others		Hunger for Power and Control
Leadership		Lone-Ranger Tactics

Jim Collins in *Good to Great*[5] defines a similar concept in his description of a Level-5 Leader. In Collins' terms, this is a leader who possesses both humility and will.

What does this mean for you?

- If you want to be seen as a leader who *gets it*, you must show ego strength *and* high levels of modesty.

- Because ego strength and modesty are independent dimensions, they can operate simultaneously. This can make you complex in the eyes of people who prefer to stereotype you simplistically. Ultimately, you will be respected if you show these diverse qualities predictably and consistently.

- If you are arrogant, instead of toning down your ego strength, you must enhance your modesty. If modesty is not natural to you, you will find it difficult to be successful as a manager or leader. Although some arrogant leaders achieve

15

positions of power, the damage and cost they create are significant.

- If you are too much of a follower, rather than flirt with arrogance, you must amplify your ego strength. If ego strength is not natural to you, you will find it difficult to be successful as a manager or leader.

- Balanced ego strength and modesty allow you to be "appropriately unreasonable," i.e., to push your staff and peers beyond their self-imposed limitations (see Chapter 4).

By the way, modesty and our core theme of simplicity have an interesting overlap. "Simple" can mean "free from guile and vanity, humble position." Innocent. Open. Modest. People who are modest see the world through unfettered eyes. They are real, not corrupted by a personal agenda. A story to illustrate:

I once coached a VP Operations who had a rough early home life. His arrogant, abusive father traveled frequently, often returning home frustrated by another unsuccessful sale. When the father berated his family, they learned to be "chameleons" to dodge his attacks. They traded their realness for survival, so to speak. As the VP pursued his early career, he used this trait to his advantage. He avoided risk and became very effective at flying under the radar. Then after five proud, successful years in his VP position, a new CEO demanded collaboration and straight talk among staff. The VP's performance faltered. His "personal agenda" was a fear of trusting others and being himself.

This is a familiar theme to anyone who has seen colleagues overwhelmed by fear. Managers derail when they are possessed by personal demons or feel they can't be themselves. Very often, this ineffective behavior shows up as low ego strength and/or low modesty. The goal, then, is to balance your ego strength and modesty. Ideally, both traits will be equally well developed and within your natural capabilities.

Although some managers are incapable of high levels of ego strength or modesty, most managers just need to amplify real parts of themselves that have become inactive. Below are some simplified tips that may be helpful for you.

If you need to develop more EGO STRENGTH:	If you need to develop more MODESTY:
• Use a 360° survey to identify proactive behaviors that your colleagues want you to enhance.	• Read books on the topics of servant leadership, consultative selling, and active listening. Apply the techniques.
• Rewrite your job description and annual objectives to reflect assertive, risk-embracing behavior.	• Simply listen more.
• Follow the tips in this chapter relating to "putting a stake in the ground" and "developing your signature style."	• Use a 360° survey to identify modesty behaviors that your colleagues want you to enhance. When you debrief your staff on your survey, apologize for past clumsiness.
• Go public with a proposal to implement an idea in which you strongly believe.	• Use Chapter 4 of this book to improve your influence skills.
• Apply the techniques in later chapters relating to managing upward, sideward, and downward.	• Find a professional coach or counselor to help identify your core values and inner barriers to modesty.
• Take a stand-up skills seminar and rehearse presentations until you *own* the material.	• Listen some more.
• Listen to energizing music or motivating books during your morning commute.	• Always ask at least 2 questions before giving a strong opinion.
• Ask your manager what it takes to exceed expectations. Then do it. Success breeds success.	• Do an unexpected favor for another department once a month.
• Attend intensive experiential training programs that challenge your self-concept.[6]	• Drop in to chat with your direct reports periodically, letting them set the agenda for the conversation.
• Engage a personal coach to help you identify breakthrough strategies for short-term performance and long-term career goals.	• Publicly give credit to your staff for their accomplishments …often.
	• Smile and lighten up.
	• Downplay your job title, perks, or power/authority.
	• Listen some more.

Put Your Stake in the Ground, Firmly

> *"Being responsible sometimes means pissing people off. ... Trying to get everyone to like you is a sign of mediocrity. Ironically, you'll simply ensure that the only people you'll wind up angering are the most creative and productive people in the organization."*

—Former Secretary of State Gen. Colin Powell

Nothing frustrates upper management more quickly than indecision. Anyone who *gets it* is decisive and expects others to be the same.

Decisiveness comes more naturally to some than others. Some managers are more suited for thorough analysis than for making quick decisions; they may be thoughtful but not quick to take a position. They are great risk managers, not risk takers. They may withhold their opinions in the company of stronger personalities. Unfortunately, even bright and talented managers can be underestimated if they spend too much time sitting on the fence.

Justin was a Controller at a fast-growing government contractor. He was known for producing accurate, timely financials. In fact, he was one of the most respected analysts in the organization, achieving a reputation at the corporate office as the go-to person to interpret P&L's. At the same time, Justin was conservative and perfectionistic. He prided himself in evaluating all angles of an issue, constantly looking for optimal solutions. He understood the business, even the strategic drivers, but this was not apparent to upper management, who never saw Justin express a personal opinion. After ten years of being passed over for promotions, a disgruntled Justin left the company.

Imagine how Justin's career might have been different if he had developed a more decisive stance on issues. Of course, he should not have tried to operate inauthentically, but even if his natural style remained conservative and analytical, he could have applied one or more of these proven techniques:

- Practice your material before stand-up presentations until you know it cold, avoiding any hint of indecisiveness or uncertainty. It's OK to confidently admit that you don't have an answer, but NEVER waffle!

- Make a list of every current, controversial issue facing the organization and develop a clear opinion on it. (This approach of "articulating a defensible point of view" is addressed in more detail in Chapter 3.)

- Read what your boss reads. Review your upcoming decisions in light of your boss's interests.

- Avoid all forms of indecision. If you don't have the information to commit to a course of action, position your opinion as, "Given what I know, I'd go with option B."

- If you ever get stuck making a decision and don't have all the facts you want, ask yourself how your most talented, decisive colleagues would proceed. If you still need more analysis, communicate a specific date when you will make the decision. Never extend this deadline.

- If you make a mistake or if your strongly held opinion is proven wrong, admit it quickly, briefly, and publicly.

Putting your stake in the ground is similar to amplifying your ego strength. By developing a strong position, you will tend to do things *your way*. In turn, you will be more respected by others who expect you to be real. And it will feel good!

Develop Your Signature Style

So far in this chapter, we have outlined methods to help you operate more authentically by understanding how you are "naturally wired." By doing this, you can more easily develop ego-modesty balance and decisiveness.

If you are successful, people will take notice. They will see that you *get it*. But a few compelling moves are not enough; you must permanently "brand" your newfound style in the mindsets of your colleagues, especially upper management. When you do this, you become memorable. You brand yourself by standing above the crowd, consistently. People assume that you *get it*, even if you are still learning.

From my lens as an executive coach, people impress me when they operate with a sense of ease and enjoyment. They are real, behaving consistently with their core values. Looking back at the values worksheet you completed earlier in this chapter, you may have already defined your natural style. Of course, some of your core values may be unproductive, in light of your business objectives or culture; other values are likely to be highly productive.

Rather than suppressing unproductive values, we prefer to coach managers to do the opposite...to amplify their productive values. In other words, it is easier to enhance than stifle your basic nature—and more fun. Think of your values as a collection of priorities deep within you, constantly competing for dominance. For instance, you may have two potentially conflicting values, "fairness to your staff" and "breakthrough performance." If fairness is too dominant, you will compromise performance. You must amplify your "breakthrough" values to create the results you want.

> *I once coached a Director of Engineering, Bob, who led a team to develop a desperately needed new product, now behind schedule. The CEO was applying enormous pressure. To his credit, Bob valued performance, delivery, timeliness, and meeting commitments. But he valued other things more— politeness, reasonable excuses, and respect for an engineer's self-motivation. As a result, he often rescued people, worked 70-hour weeks, and was burning out. During the coaching, we identified his core values and brainstormed ways to amplify the more proactive ones. We encouraged him to "do it his way" and have fun. He first printed the project due date on hats, t-shirts, and a 30-foot banner on the wall. He then found music that "juiced" his energy, playing it in the car and at work. He wrote a short mission statement for his leadership style and kept it within eyeshot. All this gave him the courage to provide more assertive feedback to his people. A few people were replaced. The team lit on fire. The project was delivered on time.*

Here is the key—because Bob already possessed the right performance values, it was possible for him to amplify them. He would not have changed if he hadn't possessed the right values in the first place. Deep down, Bob always *got it* but temporarily lost it in the face of a stressful assignment.

Think for a minute about the most productive, successful people you know. Why are they successful? In most cases, these people are driven by several core values upon which they consistently focus. Often, these values powerfully complement each other. For example, some managers are driven by both analysis and competitiveness. When both traits are equally valued, the result is a style that manages risk as it strives for growth. A different example is a manager who is driven by both collaboration and debate, resulting in a style that is trusting but insistent upon shrewd decisions. Managers in both of these examples can be successful because they operate naturally. They don't try to be someone they're not. And they have fun being themselves.

> *A division President, Sam, asked us to help him improve his leadership effectiveness in advance of a 30% annual growth plan. After reviewing his business challenges, personal goals, and 360° feedback, Sam determined that his style was too empowering. He needed to be more directive, at least until he upgraded staff and business processes. We helped him dig into his core values. Not surprisingly, he identified values such as trust, fairness, respect, and delegation. This was the way he wanted to be treated by his manager and the way he preferred to treat his people. We also identified more result-focused values such as competitiveness, perfectionism, and need for achievement—typical of top executives. Among other exercises, we asked Sam to rewrite his job description "on steroids," to identify how to amplify his results-focused values. Over the next 6 months, Sam shifted his style in a way that was real to him, focusing mostly on his competitive desire to win.*

That was three years ago. Sam first became more demanding and "edgy," something that his staff actually appreciated. Once the company achieved its financial goals, Sam was easily able to return to a more empowering style. He had developed more versatility in his leadership, amplifying different approaches in different situations. He now has a reputation for being one of the strongest leaders in his industry, constantly getting calls from recruiters who know that he *gets it.*

Recently, my partner, Jeff Grip, conducted a study of CEOs to understand how top leaders create performance breakthroughs and where they learned to do it. One glaring pattern emerged in the data— successful leaders do not all use the same methods. There is no magic formula known only to members of the CEO Club. Breakthrough leaders tend to develop a natural style early in career and stick with it. They play to their strengths, so to speak, with little concern for comparing their styles with others'.

So here's a sobering thought: What if your natural style or core values do not match what is required to do your job? Or what if you are competent but not having fun?

Kim advanced quickly as an IT manager in Fortune 100 companies, not because of her technical acumen but more from her love of strategy and leadership. She eventually landed a CIO position in a smaller $80m company. The position was a hands-on fix-it assignment with minimal staff. Kim had the skills, but her core values were not a natural fit. She started to spend excess time developing long-term business strategies, something she enjoyed. Her department botched an ERP conversion because Kim did not keep her eye on the ball. Kim left the company, not on her own accord.

Although Kim was talented, this experience was painful and costly to both Kim and her employer. She should have stayed on a strategic CIO path in a larger company or switched to a general management track earlier in her career.

To thrive in your career, you must be brutally honest with yourself about your natural talents and whether you are enjoying yourself. If you are thoughtful, you can select a career path that fits. No job or path is a perfect fit, and everyone has some degree of mismatch. The most important thing is to be honest with yourself about your real skills and abilities. This, in turn, allows you the choice to follow a career path or redesign your job to reflect what comes naturally.

"Don't be afraid of being unique. It's like being afraid of your best self."

—Donald Trump

Recap

Getting it requires you to be "real." The first step is to understand and openly admit your naturally occurring skills, abilities, and core values...including your flaws. It is easiest to perform if you operate within your natural range. Being real also requires you to show ego-modesty balance and a high degree of decisiveness. As you become more comfortable in your own skin and operate *your way*, you develop a signature style that is spontaneous, sincere, and real to others. Ultimately, you gain a reputation for *getting it*.

Chapter 3

Exceed Expectations

*"When someone exceeds my expectations, I remember
it for a long, long time."*

—Any CEO

This topic needs little introduction. Obviously, your manager wants you to exceed his or her expectations. This is easier said than done, as you know. The secret is not to "wow" management with elaborate schemes or overpromised goals. You are most impressive when you focus on simple fundamentals such as the six outlined in this chapter.

Warning Signs of Not Exceeding Expectations

- Your manager has unstated expectations and you don't know exactly what they are.

- You find yourself struggling to converse at the right level of detail.

- You don't understand why senior executives get so upset when unavoidable surprises occur.

Understand Your Manager's Core Values

In Chapter 2, you explored your values to develop an authentic style of operating. Being real helps you to be compelling. Similarly, understanding your manager's values will help you to be compelling in a different way. If you know what makes your manager tick, you can more easily exceed your manager's expectations of you. This is especially true if your manager is hard to read or predict.

If you are lucky, your manager is real, with an open, transparent style. What you see is what you get. Unfortunately, few bosses are this easy. Like most people, they often work hard to present a positive image, especially if they are in a visible position of leadership. They either project an image that conforms to the culture of the business or to their view of what will gain others' approval. Even if they are straightforward and have high integrity, it is human nature for them to spin their image to some degree.

Your manager's values, not the image he or she maintains or the words he or she speaks, are the best predictors of what he or she expects. As such, you must understand these oft-hidden values if you hope to truly *get* your manager.

> *Denise thought she had a great manager. When she first interviewed with the firm, her manager-to-be talked at length about the company's people-oriented, empowered culture. Denise was sure that this was the kind of organization where she could perform because she truly felt supported. After she was hired, Denise noticed that her manager got easily frustrated over small mistakes, often to the point of overcontrol and verbal abuse. Eventually, it dawned on Denise that her manager, in reality, was a closet autocrat.*

Although Denise's manager appeared to value empowerment, he valued other things more—micromanaging and venting his frustrations without regard for his impact.

It is almost impossible to determine your manager's values by asking what those values are. This is especially true when you interview for a new position, with everyone putting on their best faces. You can't assume that your manager truly values his publicly stated objectives and priorities. Worse yet, your manager may be oblivious to his own values, because they are often unconscious. The best way to determine a person's values is to infer them, as we illustrated in Chapter 2, from three types of consistent behavior observed over time—habits, emotional reactions, and investment of time and/or money.

You can use the worksheet on the following page to brainstorm your manager's core values. To make this more interesting, in the first section, you can make a list of your manager's *spoken* beliefs and priorities. This will allow you to identify gaps where your manager may not be "walking the talk."

It takes psychological savvy to infer a person's core values from his or her behavioral patterns. Sometimes the links are obvious, and

Worksheet to Brainstorm Your Manager's Core Values

List examples of your manager's spoken beliefs and priorities, which may not reflect his or her core values:	
List examples of your manager's *habitual behavior*, those things that he or she does repeatedly and consistently at work. This includes tasks that are most enjoyable to your manager, and those things he or she has a reputation for doing.	Stemming from the patterns of behavior in the left column, what appear to be your manager's underlying values?
List any *emotional reactions* your manager has shown at work in the past year. These could be positive emotions or negative emotions (joy, excitement, frustration, anger, apprehension).	
List how your manager spends most of his or her *time* and *money* at work.	

sometimes not. If you are thoughtful and patient, over time, you'll become more skilled. Even if you can't fully glean your manager's underlying values, this analysis can at least help you better predict his or her patterns.

If you are unfortunate to have a dysfunctional manager, a values analysis may reduce your frustration. The less frustrated you are, the more willing and able you are to exceed your manager's expectations, even if those expectations are quirky.

Here are some further tips that can help you understand your manager:

- Remember that you can't change anyone's core values. You need to accept your manager, warts and all, or go find another job.

- When you promote an idea to your manager, you must satisfy your manager's unspoken values, not just his or her stated priorities. For example, your manager may say she is ready to invest in new capital for your department but has a history of penny-pinching. This tells you that you must always lead your argument with cost-savings data.

- If your manager's values are dysfunctional, your options for exceeding his or her expectations may be limited. Fortunately, in most organizations, justice eventually prevails. Eventually, you will get a better manager, or maybe YOU will get to be the manager!

- If your manager has a complex set of values, this is an advantage to you. Your manager may be hard to understand, but once you figure him or her out, you can then advise your peers on how to exceed your manager's expectations. This reinforces the fact to everyone involved that you *get it*.

- Once you appreciate that most members of upper management have an underlying set of values, you will feel more comfortable relating to them. Rather than being wowed by their status or frustrated by their seemingly irrational behavior, you will see them as complex and inevitably flawed...similar to you and me.

The most successful managers make it a disciplined practice to observe people's behavior to interpret their underlying values. If you practice, over time you will become more persuasive and influential with all members of upper management. Because most of your peers don't do this, you will have a distinct advantage.

"I (look to hire people with) a passionate curiosity...alert and very awake and engaged with the world and wanting to know more."[1]

—Nell Minow, former President, Institutional Shareholder Services

What if Your Boss is the CEO?

If your manager happens to be the CEO or a strong-willed Division President, you will enjoy this section. It outlines some of the unique qualities found in people who are "wired" to reach the top. Even if the chief executive is a couple levels above you, you should understand how he or she thinks and how to exceed his or her expectations.

Although it is true that CEOs put their pants on one leg at a time, in many ways, they are very different from 99.9% of the people walking the face of the earth. This is visible very early in a career. The following quip is only partly tongue-in-cheek:

We've developed a foolproof test to predict whether people have what it takes to be a CEO. When they reach age 18, we simply ask them if they would ever want the job. If they hesitate for a second, they're not it.

There are two areas in which CEOs are distinguished from mere mortals. One relates to talent, and the other relates to—you guessed it—values. Let's first talk about talent, which we'll define as innate ability. Since the mid-1980s, our executive assessment practice has taught us that successful CEOs have abilities such as intellectual speed, conceptual skill, competitiveness, perfectionism, ego strength, and modesty. Because these abilities are clearly evident from an early age, we can assume that they are genetically determined, not learned.

These qualities alone don't define a CEO. The highest-performing VPs, middle managers, and nonmanaging professionals have these same abilities. What seems to differentiate CEOs is their value system. A CEO study we conducted in the 1990s[2] revealed that most successful CEOs tend to share the following deeply seated values. The percentage of our sample possessing each value is noted in parentheses:

- Constant need for intellectual stimulation (85%)

- Drive for personal achievement (77%)

- Perfectionistic desire for competence and efficiency (73%)

These values were much more prevalent than other values that emerged in the study, such as:

- Maintaining open communication with others (50%)

- Teaching, coaching, and mentoring (12%)

- Achieving family balance (8%)

This doesn't mean that successful CEOs are cutthroat mercenaries, but that success requires intense personal ambition and extraordinary standards. The company literally becomes an extension of the CEO's self. Family is much less important than career. Even though some researchers would say that CEO values have become more balanced in recent years, I know of few CEOs who achieve the level of family balance that their families secretly desire.

What about the low percentages found for "open communication" and "coaching" in our study? Even though it is commonly accepted that the best CEOs are terrific communicators and devote significant time to coaching, these appear to be secondary values. Most CEOs communicate only when there is a result-based benefit. If you have a CEO who is a great communicator/coach, I'll bet you $100 that they would rather be scrutinizing a puzzling P&L or eviscerating a competitor. It requires a conscious, disciplined effort for a CEO to listen, coach, or spend time with his or her family. Such is the nature of alpha dogs.

Yes, of course, there are exceptions. Extraverts love to interact. Servant leaders, especially those over age 50, gain satisfaction from giving/coaching,[2] but the vast majority of CEOs are driven by values that are different from those of other executives. For you to understand, tolerate, and exceed the expectations of your CEO, you must understand CEOs' basic natures. To show your CEO that you *get it*, you must appreciate his or her quirks and never suffer the illusion that you can change him or her.

Another issue begs discussion. What about the concept of a signature style that we discussed in Chapter 2? Do all CEOs share a common set of characteristics, or do they possess unique, individual styles? The answer is both. In another CEO study conducted in 2007, we found that successful CEOs possess most of the talent and values characteristics outlined above.[3] We also found that CEOs tend to play one or two signature characteristics at a high volume. For example, some CEOs achieve most of their leverage with relentless perfectionism. Others get results with extreme competitiveness, talent upgrading, and/or process discipline. One reason these CEOs are successful is that they do what comes naturally, with great intensity.

Not all signature styles are appropriate for all business conditions. A steroidally competitive CEO is most effective in a competitive market. A financially-obsessed CEO is most appropriate for a private equity play with a short-term exit. A perfectionistic CEO is most effective where costs are out of control or product quality is critical. A process-disciplined CEO is best when an operations turnaround is essential.

If you want to exceed the expectations of the top executives in your company, you must understand how they think and operate differently from you. You must understand their priorities and their passions. If you can show them that you get *them*, you have an edge in getting business in general.

Learn to Fly at 30,000 Feet, Even if You're Not a Frequent Flyer

The worksheet in the appendix indicates that one type of versatility you must master is "detail versatility." This allows you to operate at either macro- or micro-levels of detail, easily and spontaneously. Although much of this trait is innate, especially at the broad level required for C-level positions, you can improve your skill. Detail versatility is essential if you seek to exceed the expectations of senior management.

In our management assessment practice, we observe that about 40% of managers tend to be stuck in a mindset that is overly detailed and technically focused. Although some managers have the opposite problem, this is relatively rare. Even vice presidents can have an exaggerated bias for details. This frustrates colleagues who are more strategic and broad-gauged.

If you are a detailed, technical thinker and show any of the signs above, you may have a credibility problem. You might operate inefficiently or may frustrate talented colleagues who leverage themselves at a higher level. Upper management will assume that you

```
┌─────────────────────────────────────────────┐
│        Warning Signs of Being Too Detailed   │
│   •  You are often verbose and take too long  │
│      to get to the point.                      │
│   •  You feel a compulsion to be thorough      │
│      when others don't really care.            │
│   •  You've been accused of being more         │
│      process-focused than result-focused.      │
└─────────────────────────────────────────────┘
```

don't *get it* if you can't pull out of the weeds. Your name may elude the succession plan if you have been stereotyped as "forever technical." Worse yet, you may find yourself promoted to a level beyond your capability.

> *A division President, Craig, was in trouble with his board because he was not developing a compelling strategy for the business. When he asked if I wanted to see his annual board presentation, scheduled for the next week, I readily agreed. Craig led me into a large conference room with 50 pages taped to the wall. As he outlined his detailed presentation, it became clear that his approach was to take 60 minutes to lead his board to a final conclusion. I interrupted him to suggest that he put the last slide first and cut the presentation to 15 slides. When he looked at me, puzzled, I thought to myself, "Houston, we have a problem. He doesn't get it."*

This diagram may help evaluate if you are limited to a narrow range of detail. Ask yourself where you spend most of your time.

30,000 feet	Detail Versatility		1,000 feet
Visionary	**Strategic**	**Functional**	**Technical**

Of course, your ultimate goal is to be versatile enough to maneuver the whole spectrum at will; however, the most common challenge for managers is to avoid getting fixated at the technical or functional level. Assuming that you have the talent and your values support the development of detail versatility, here are six strategies that you can pursue, roughly in this sequence:

1. Eliminate tactical behaviors in situations where you must be strategic. For example, when you run into your CEO and he asks, "How's it going?" limit your response to one sentence, not an exhaustive project update. Similarly, keep standup presentations short and macro, but have lots of detail in your back pocket.

2. Observe the specific behaviors of the most strategic thinkers in your organization. Copy them shamelessly.

3. If you ever notice yourself conversing on a different wavelength with an impatient senior executive, map the conversation afterward. Go back to your office, get out a sheet of paper, and diagram the level of detail each of you displayed during the conversation. You will likely find that you kept pulling the conversation in a micro direction while the other person kept trying to pull to a more macro level. In addition, you were likely moving slowly and they were likely moving quickly.

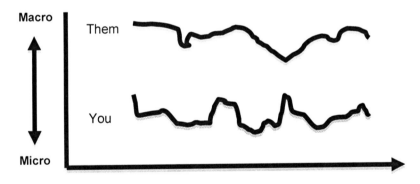

Conversation over Time

4. Read more strategic books and articles. Find out what upper management is reading.

5. Request mentoring from your manager and/or other strategic thinkers. Most accomplished executives are flattered to be asked for advice. Keep it simple, such as, "Linda, you are much better at strategic thinking than I am.

Could I buy you lunch a couple times this year to pick your brain?"

6. Seek job rotations. If you are really serious about advancing to upper management, your resume will be much more impressive if you have two different functions under your belt by the time you hit mid career. More importantly, you will gain experience that will broaden your thinking, your network, and your execution skills.

Articulate Defensible Points of View

"To be compelling to senior management you must have a defensible point of view."

—Gary Graves, Chairman, Caribou Coffee Company

In Chapter 2, we discussed the importance of putting a stake in the ground, developing a decisive mindset. In this section, the emphasis is on knowledge of critical business issues, debating them confidently with senior management. If you show thoughtfulness and the courage to speak your mind, senior management will see that you *get it*.

This skill requires knowledge. The more informed you are on relevant business issues, the more you will be seen by upper management as worthy of their attention. Relevant knowledge varies by industry, current market challenges, and the personal interests of your leaders. In general, you should have a working knowledge of:

- Market and technology trends that impact customer priorities, competitor strategy, and product development.

- Economic climate that impacts investor confidence, investment capital, and customer budgets.

- Philosophical and strategic pressures from the corporate office.

- Customers' perceptions of your company's performance.

- Process improvement approaches designed to improve efficiency and cost.

- The pros and cons of your organization's metrics (finance and productivity) and the degree to which systems data is credible.

- Supply chain issues and opportunities.

- How others perceive you and your staff in terms of talent and execution skills.

It is your responsibility to be well read and well informed. Most importantly, you must understand the controversies within your business and the motivations of the people involved in them. This includes the diverse viewpoints of all members of the executive team. If you are to develop points of view that are defensible, you can't rely on a superficial or popular understanding. You must develop a deep curiosity about your business and understand it on more than one or two dimensions.

Once you know your material, the second step is articulation. People judge your thinking by your speech. You can't be long-winded, micro-focused or misuse grammar and vocabulary. You must exceed the expectations of your audience.

Here are some techniques than can help you to be more articulate with senior management:

1. Remember that people are more preoccupied with their interests than yours. You must become skilled at capturing their attention in fewer than 10 seconds. If they are impatient, typical of top executives, you have only 5 seconds.

2. Rather than talk fast, you must talk less. Your words must be efficient.

3. To be compelling, you must be confident. Eliminate tentative words (such as maybe, sometimes, perhaps, a little, and might) from your vocabulary.

4. You must appeal to WIIFT, or "what's in it for them." If you understand their viewpoints (and values!) ahead of time, you can frame your ideas in their language.

5. You need to fly at the same altitude, as outlined in the previous section. If they ascend to 30,000 feet or swoop down to 1,000 feet, follow them.

I Get It!

6. During a debate, most people mistakenly stop listening in an attempt to position their own ideas. Your most powerful tool is active listening. This means that you need to ask questions, restate the other person's ideas and let the other person do most of the talking.

7. If the discussion gets emotional, don't polarize to an opposite viewpoint. Often, the best way to defend your point of view is to show the other person that you understand his or hers. Then simply say that the two of you are not in sync.

The point here is not to win arguments or to be right. It is merely to communicate in a manner that earns you respect as an intellectual peer. Senior executives will assume that you *get it* if you can articulate clear, defensible opinions.

Stay Focused in the Face of Being Overwhelmed

"The average American worker has fifty interruptions a day, of which seventy percent have nothing to do with work."

—W. Edwards Deming

According to Robertt Young, productivity coach with the Effective Edge in Austin, Texas, an average manager encounters about 200 new pieces of information each day. A recent study showed 50% more paper in offices than a decade ago, suggesting that the paperless office is not coming soon. Four out of five documents that we keep, we never refer to again. The average manager spends 150 hours per year looking for misplaced information.

Today, everyone struggles with information overload and distractions. It's the nature of an increasingly complex world. Losing focus has both short-term and long-term costs. Short-term, you may do the wrong tasks, or do them inefficiently. Long-term, you can risk your job and your reputation. It is hard to exceed your manager's expectations when you are scrambling to keep up.

Some people are more naturally focused than others. Think about colleagues who always seem to be purposeful, efficient, and clear-minded. They never appear frazzled, nor do they complain about workloads. They don't make frequent jokes about being out of control.

34

They accomplish an extraordinary amount of work in a short period of time. And they get the right stuff done.

Naturally organized people are the fortunate few. I once worked with Bob Ableidinger, CEO of the Hollinee Corporation. He ran a $100M company with five GMs worldwide, two financial people, two phone lines, a fax machine, and no secretary. And he worked with a clean desk! His simplicity was stunning, as was his success. He *got it* and operated in a way that fit his natural style.

On the opposite pole, unfocused managers tend to firefight rather than plan. They multitask haphazardly, often doubling back to rework problems. They are likely to complain and blame others for their plight. They are both visibly and invisibly stressed. Although some of these managers are out of control because they are "Peter principled" beyond their capability, most simply need to learn technique. Fortunately, advice is readily available and not difficult to adopt.

Christina Randle, founder of the Effective Edge, has developed a variety of practical methods that are outlined in her book, *Getting It Together.*[4] Other experts such as David Allen[5] discuss similar principles. There are basically three strategies used by effective managers to maintain maximum focus:

1. Clear the decks.

2. Manage your inputs.

3. Act on priorities.

Strategy 1—Clear the decks

A lion tamer takes three things into the cage: a whip, a gun, and a chair. We know what the whip and gun are for. The chair, it turns out, confuses the lion, as he tries to focus on all four legs at once. When lions get confused, they become passive and easy to control.

Before you can effectively manage the bazillion inputs you receive, you must limit the number of distractions in front of you at any one time. Your workspace and mind must be uncluttered. Your thoughts and actions must flow, unencumbered. You must not be passive and easy to control by others.

Typical techniques for clearing the decks include the following:

- Purge old files and stacks.

- Toss or shred everything outdated.

- Relabel and file your reference documents, delegating to an assistant if possible.

- Relabel your action files (projects, clients/customers, other current work).

Then comes the hard part, often requiring a professional coach: You need a system to track your action items. Historically, people used a to-do list or planner/diary. Today, most people use Outlook® or LotusNotes®. The pros and cons of these systems are not hard to figure out, but a coach can help you pick a system that matches your natural style. By the way, the best systems do not use A/B/C priorities that constantly change. Rather, if you continually identify only one *next action* for each of your complex projects, your list may be short enough that priorities are evident.

Another pointer: Work with a clean desk, like my friend Bob. Yes, even if you are a "piler." Put piles on a credenza behind you if you must. Studies have shown that every additional distraction in your visual field steals a portion of your focus. Thus, if you have numerous files and papers on your desk, you could be working at less than 50% focus! Ideally, your desk will have an in-box, out-box, phone, perhaps a lamp, and lots of empty space on which to work the ONE most pressing priority at a time.

Strategy 2—Manage your inputs

Inputs come from many angles. Phone calls. Emails. Mail. Memos. Reports. Post-its. Most experts recommend that you handle one thing at a time, whether dealing with email, voicemail, or in-box items. With each input, make one of the following four decisions in the moment:

- Dump It—Trash it or file it (remember, 80% of what we keep is never referred to again).

- Do It—If you can handle it in less than two minutes, do it now!

- Delegate It—Ask, "who else should do this instead of me?"

- Defer It—Put it on your calendar or to-do list.

With emails, your goal is to clear them out, perhaps once an hour, using the decision rules above. I don't have to tell you how good it feels to have an empty in-box, even for an hour! Most organized managers use electronic folders to organize their incoming emails. This is effective as long as you link them to the appropriate next-action tasks.

Strategy 3—Act on priorities

This is a difficult strategy for most, because it requires more than simply setting up a good system. You must *want* to use the system. As we discovered in Chapter 2, adopting a new behavior is easy if the behavior aligns with your core values. You simply read a book on best practices and apply them immediately.

If, however, deep down, you don't value self-discipline, you will revert to old habits that are ineffective. For example, let's say you love short-term tactical stimulation, like many stressed managers. It is therefore easier and more fun to pile things on your desk, even if you consistently lose them. This leads to the treadmill of, "Where the heck did I put that thing?...I'll call Joe later while I look for it....Oops, I forgot to forward these documents....Here come ten more emails....Maybe I should print them out and put them in another pile...."

For those of you who don't value self-discipline or who thrive on multitasking, the best approach is to experiment with techniques until you find something that fits you. Below are some promising techniques you can try.

1. If your boss sets effective priorities, copy the same methods to see if they work for you.

2. Set up each of your projects, or tasks that have more than one step, as a single task in Outlook® or LotusNotes®. The title should be "ProjectName—NextAction," with all the subsequent actions hidden in the detail window. As each action is completed, simply retitle the task with the next action. This way, your to-do list has fewer items, all reflecting top-priority actions.

3. Don't keep your email application as the front window on your computer. Put your to-do list in front, instead. Set your email program to receive new emails hourly, avoiding

constant tactical interruptions. This keeps you in control of your priorities rather than having other people whipsaw you.

4. Color-code and sort your to-do tasks according to categories such as Actions, Projects, Calls, Waiting For, and Someday Maybe. A great system is outlined in detail in Randle's book,[4] and her organization offers online training for users of Outlook® (www.effectiveedge.com).

5. Forget all the computer systems and planners if you are not a technology person. Simply make lists with a pad of paper. We once knew a CEO of a $600M company who required all his managers to use this simple approach. It worked amazingly well.

Avoid Surprises at All Costs

This fundamental is pretty straightforward but easy to forget. If you ask any seasoned senior executive what frustrates him or her most, "surprises" falls in the top ten. CEOs all put it in their top three. Most don't even like positive surprises.

Alan ran an $800M manufacturing division of a $10B corporation. Because of an up-cycle in their industry, Alan's company was producing more profit than any other division by a factor of three. This alone put Alan on the corporate radar screen, but he got even more attention because he was exceeding plan by 30%. Rather than being happy, the corporate CEO was convinced that because Alan couldn't forecast accurately, he couldn't control his business. Alan's CEO didn't like surprises.

Top executives hate surprises for a number of reasons:

• The shareholders' mantra is "meet commitments."

• Appearing out of control can cost CEOs six-figure bonuses, or their jobs.

• A failure can ruin a reputation.

• In a world of uncertainty, a sense of control simply feels good.

38

It isn't too hard to avoid surprises. Simply keep your boss informed, frequently, good news and bad. But some bosses don't make it easy. They may be inconsistent in their priorities or focus. They may, for example, get upset on Monday about financials, saying, "I want to see budget variances on a weekly basis," but then the next Monday, ask you why you are wasting their time with unnecessary reporting. Other senior managers, especially CEOs, may give mixed signals about the level of detail they expect in communication. They may impatiently fly at 30,000 feet during the first half of a management review, then suddenly deep-dive to a microanalysis of product features or budgets.

Most of the time, thankfully, senior managers are driven by common sense and consistency. As such, the rules for avoiding surprises are straightforward:

1. First, ask your boss outright what kinds of surprises are worst.

2. Next, evaluate your boss's values and infer what kind of information he or she prefers. Pay special attention to past cases in which your boss was surprised and became emotional.

3. If metrics are weak in your department, work with your manager to create simple, sensible measures of performance and report them in a way your manager prefers.

4. Figure out how much informal communication your manager wants. Just ask. Some impatient managers may give signals that they don't want to be bothered but are, in reality, hungry for you to stop in informally for quick chats. Don't overuse email with these people.

5. Err in the direction of overcommunication if you see a potential risk. Always propose an action or solution, rather than simply blow a whistle.

6. If you have thin skin, beware. Your career is in danger, literally, if you develop a reputation for dodging straight talk when a real danger faces the business. Top executives depend heavily on people like you who are close to the action, especially if they are preoccupied elsewhere.

I Get It!

Recap

To *get it* in the eyes of your manager and other executives, you must exceed their expectations, including their stated and unstated expectations. By discerning their core values, you can learn to satisfy what they really want, even if they are not consciously aware of it. Understanding the unique talents and values of the CEO is required if you must interact with the top dog. One way to exceed expectations is to think, and talk, in macro-strategic terms rather than getting caught up in inappropriate detail. Another way is to articulate defensible points of view, showing that you are informed and articulate. You must also remain focused on key priorities. Finally, it is critical to avoid surprises, showing that you are in control of your world.

Chapter 4

Create Accountability

As the story goes, the ancient Romans had a tradition. Whenever one of their engineers designed an arch, the engineer assumed accountability for his work in the most profound way possible—when the capstone was set in place, he stood underneath.

> **Warning Signs of Lack of Accountability**
> - Your staff joke about going home early.
> - Your staff tend to focus solely on their own jobs, saying that what happens in other departments is out of their control.
> - At the end of the year, you have a hard time justifying your performance reviews.

Accountability occurs when your staff willingly take full responsibility for their commitments. Accountability is a natural outcome when you surround yourself with high-talent people who gain satisfaction from rallying behind a challenging plan. They know exactly what is expected of them and how they will be measured. They not only are accountable but badly WANT to be accountable. They are engaged. You can create accountability and engagement by mastering the five fundamentals outlined below.

Upgrade Talent as if Your Career Depended on It

You must have high levels of talent on your team to create full accountability. When any of your people lack capacity or ability, they become too preoccupied with their own plight to be concerned about meeting commitments to you or others. If you spend time rescuing them, you have less time to focus on more value-added activities such as planning or developing cross-functional relationships. Literally, your career depends on the caliber of your people.

If you inherit a new team, you will likely need to upgrade a few positions, especially if your predecessor didn't *get* the importance of talent. Even if you have managed your team for a while, some people's abilities are likely being stretched because of increasing demands on the business. Whereas the "Peter Principle"[1] says that people tend to get promoted to their levels of incompetence, nowadays, incompetence can occur even if people stay in place! In our talent-assessment practice, we typically find that 10–20% of a team's members show a talent gap. Your prime directive must be to hire, promote, and assertively develop a team of stars. You must do this proactively, with high urgency.

> *William joined an engineered-products company as its new product development VP. His charter was to upgrade the talent of legacy engineers and managers to meet new customer demands. The group had long succeeded on the coattails of classic, low-tech products. Engineers performed a familiar maintenance function, tweaking designs at a slow pace. Even though William suspected that only 50% of the group was capable and motivated, he spent more than 12 months trying to educate and develop the laggards. He figured that with continued coaching, they would pick up the pace. It was not until three customers departed and the president offered William an exit package that he finally understood the urgency.*

Some business models say that before you can upgrade talent, you must know what kind of talent the business plan requires and how your organization should be structured. Unfortunately, if you wait for the annual planning cycle, you can fall behind. Upgrading talent must be an ongoing endeavor, especially during times of change. Upgrading is daily hygiene, not a discrete event.

"The team with the best players wins."

—Jack Welch, former Chairman, GE

Of course you can't define headcount without a clue as to upcoming business demands. You can't always predict the future knowledge and skills required for each position; however, 99% of the time, you can assume that your business is becoming more complex and faster paced. Critical positions therefore require accelerated talent, particularly the dimension of VERSATILITY.

Let's look at how versatility applies to your staff. "Versatile" means "capable of or adapted for changing easily between various tasks or fields of endeavor; having or capable of many uses." If your staff are versatile, they adapt to change. They are ready for rotations, cross-training, and unfamiliar assignments. They handle uncertainty without fear. They may be more promotable. Not surprisingly, versatile people perform consistently at a high level.

Since the 1980s, our consulting firm has assessed the talent of thousands of managers and executives. We have used numerous competency profiles to define high performance. We have studied how high-potential managers perform, across multiple industries. From this experience, we have isolated ten traits that are predictive of versatility, illustrated on the next page. If you can develop a team that possesses these traits, it is likely to perform, no matter the business conditions.

These ten versatility traits comprise a simplified list. Of course there are times when additional competencies should be assessed. For instance, technical positions require technical knowledge. Customer-service positions require product knowledge and communication skills. Leadership positions may require change-management skill, business acumen, or strategic aptitude. Learning to identify and assess most competencies is fairly straightforward. Assessing versatility traits is more difficult but ultimately powerful.

To assess the versatility of your staff, you need data. As with any talent assessment, data should be triangulated from multiple sources. These could include past performance reviews, 360° surveys, customer feedback, job simulations, interviews, and input from HR. You may need a professional assessment from an organizational psychologist for some of the ten traits on our Versatility Checklist. Once you have sufficient data, the worksheet in the appendix can help you determine whether the overall versatility of an employee is low, moderate, or high.

Stella was Sales VP at a large equipment-leasing company. Her team had always performed, but the industry was becoming more competitive. Revenues and margins were slipping. With the help of her HR VP, Stella first reevaluated customer needs and the skills her group required to exceed them. She asked her peers to help rate the versatility of each manager on her team, using the

VERSATILITY TRAITS

Intellectual Versatility	
Conceptual Thinking	Thinks abstractly to grasp complex, multidimensional problems. Is not black-and-white. Tolerates ambiguity.
Mental Focus	Maintains mental focus through a long conversation or a long project. Prioritizes effectively.
Detail Versatility	Thinks at an appropriate level of detail, either macro or micro. Can go from 30,000 feet to 1,000 feet, and vice versa, "at will."
Decisiveness/Drive	Takes risks. Is decisive without overanalyzing or hesitating. Shows healthy impatience and urgency.
Social Versatility	
Social Insight	Reads the points of view and feelings of others, including his or her own impact on others. Has "emotional intelligence."
Confidence-Modesty Balance	Shows strength in BOTH areas: • Confidence—Addresses challenging tasks or people without hesitation. • Modesty—Self-effaces, maintains others' self-esteem (no arrogance).
Listening	Patiently puts own agenda aside to embrace another's. Asks questions. Seeks to understand.
Leadership Versatility	
Integrity	Values candor. Admits mistakes. Respects compliance and regulatory requirements. Acts professionally.
Delegation	Willing to give up control. Empowers people with responsibility and authority. Leverages own efforts through others.
Accountability	Holds people accountable to their commitments. Values results more than getting people's approval.

versatility traits that she deemed as applying to sales management. She spent half of her time over the next three months coaching her lowest-versatility managers to give them a fair shake at development. By six months, 10% improved their skills markedly, 20% resigned voluntarily, and 30% were transferred to less-demanding sales roles. The next fiscal year, her team documented a $100M increase in revenues.

Was Stella's approach too harsh? Absolutely not, considering the urgency in the market and Stella's thoughtful, fair style. Even though some of the "casualties" of this upgrading were not happy, i.e., they didn't *get it*, most were relieved and thankful to escape the pressure of an increasingly demanding job.

A few words are appropriate here on the topic of equal opportunity and the legal side of staffing. Basically, the EEOC guidelines[2] and the Civil Rights Act[3] prohibit discrimination on the basis of race, color, religion, creed, gender, national origin, age, or disability. Compliance with these laws requires that your employee-selection procedures demonstrate "job-relatedness," meaning that employees are selected for their abilities to perform the job, not on the basis of irrelevant factors. In other words, before you make hiring or restaffing changes with any skill profile, you should be able to document, with HR support, that the skills and traits are necessary for the positions in question. If you define a competency profile and use multiple sources of assessment, your approach is highly defensible.

But don't get overconfident yet. You will inevitably encounter barriers in your efforts to upgrade your staff. The first relates to developability. Many of the ten versatility traits are not easily developable. For instance, those easiest to develop include listening, delegation skill, and holding people accountable. Most of the others are difficult or impossible to develop. Of course you should always give your people a chance to develop before making personnel changes. This requires you to master skills in giving feedback, coaching, and employee development. The ROI on development of versatility is typically low, however.

There are other barriers to talent upgrading that are even more sobering. Your biggest nightmare could a scenario in which:

- your organization values loyalty over performance, or the culture is conflict-avoidant.
- your boss and/or HR don't *get it*.

- your company has been sued over wrongful termination and/or its attorneys don't understand best-practice upgrading.

- training budgets and HR resources are limited.

Although some of these barriers may be out of your direct control, others are clearly within your influence. As you build a reputation for *getting it*, upper management will be more compelled by your upgrading plans. If you develop strong influence skills (see Chapter 5) and are armed with effective performance-management skills (feedback, coaching, development planning), you will be even more persuasive.

A high-performing organization that *gets it* will value performance over loyalty, accountability over fear. Management (and legal counsel) will understand that upgrading is legally defensible, fair to all concerned, and required to be competitive.

Clarify and Align Priorities

> *"Management is doing things right; leadership is doing the right things."*

> —Peter Drucker

In his words above, Drucker was not talking about ethics but about priorities. "Doing the right things" requires that all members of an organization align with strategic goals *and* each other. Once your team is focused in the right direction, you can hold them accountable for what really counts.

Some organizations work hard to create alignment intentionally. Other organizations are more casual about alignment, often resulting in fuzzy priorities and weak accountability. Even talented managers need to be aligned.

> *"If talented managers are not aligned, they fall victim to the 'chaos of good intentions,' going off in unfocused, albeit ambitious directions."*

> —Joe Wright, CEO, Master Chemical Corporation

If you survey 100 diverse organizations, you will find an astonishing range of approaches to defining objectives, setting priorities, and holding people accountable to meet them. Some organizations are highly formal and structured, whereas others are quite loose. In small organizations, management systems typically reflect the personal preferences of the owner or chief executive. In larger organizations, management systems result from collaboration between the senior staff and HR.

There is no single formula or best practice that applies to all organizations. Entrepreneurial organizations tend to work best with informal systems, whereas larger, more complex organizations require more formal structure. Government contractors and financial institutions are more structured because of regulatory constraints. Food, healthcare, and pharmaceutical industries have their own compliance challenges.

Although you may have little control over the design of the management systems within your company, you can certainly align priorities within your team or department. You can improve alignment within your group no matter how much structure your organization embraces. Outlined below are three practices you can follow to align your people's efforts.

1. Define objectives and metrics with an eye toward the strategic plan and cross-functional processes.

2. Write objectives to be crystal clear and as simple as possible.

3. Encourage frequent communication between people whose objectives interact.

Practice 1—Define objectives and metrics with an eye toward the strategic plan and cross-functional processes

The goal here is to define objectives and metrics in a broad context. Too often, the management by objectives (MBO) or objectives-setting process is a narrowly focused, bureaucratic dance between manager and staff. Either the manager dictates the objectives or the staff member takes the first crack. Discussion and negotiation are minimal. The focus is typically on staff members satisfying their technical roles, continuing unfinished work from the previous year, or meeting budget numbers that are dictated from upper management.

In contrast, strategically focused managers "cascade" objectives downward, starting with the business plan, then getting more specific as objectives are defined successively at lower levels. Objectives and metrics are designed to reflect, as directly as possible, strategic imperatives. In addition, the objectives of other departments are considered, to enhance process flow and cooperation. For example, let's say you are a middle manager writing your objectives for a new year. You first review the organization's strategic plan and annual objectives, along with your functional leader's and/or manager's objectives. You and your manager then work together to craft your personal objectives and metrics in a larger strategic context. During this process, you talk to peers in other functions, checking how their priorities affect you and your group. You then cascade this process to your people, helping them understand priorities of upper management and process links to cross-functional peers. Even if their objectives end up being narrow and technically focused, they will have considered the bigger picture.

Vocollect is a Pittsburgh-based distributor of voice-recognition supply-chain solutions. When authoring annual objectives, they encourage each manager to look upward and sideward. The most effective managers meet with peers to negotiate their objectives, especially where cross-functional cooperation is critical.

Many organizations have adopted Balanced Scorecards[4] to better align objectives and metrics. By balancing diverse performance metrics that apply to different functions within the business, managers learn to pay attention to broader business landscapes.

If you create alignment within your department, even if you do it under the radar of upper management, over time you will improve the focus of your people. Your staff will become more accountable to strategic imperatives and customer needs. Upper management, if they are watching, will notice that your people *get it.*

Practice 2—Write objectives to be crystal clear and as simple as possible

This is simple in concept but difficult in practice. People tend to complicate and obfuscate. In the introduction to this book, we discussed complexity and simplicity. Complexity often creates value, but complication is inefficient. Similarly, simplicity is linked to high performance, whereas being simplistic is not. The goal is to keep things as simple as possible in a world of increasing complexity without being simplistic.

"You don't have good objectives until you can explain them on a bar napkin to the bartender."

—Michael Bayles, former Group President, Quanex

The classic way to optimize complexity and simplicity is to write SMART (specific, measurable, attainable, relevant, time-bound) objectives.[5] An example of a SMART objective is "Improve inventory turns by 15% by the end of Q4" or "Generate 20% increase in organic sales growth through new program wins in the next fiscal year." Not much controversy here. If you master the SMART approach and teach your people to do the same, your objectives will be more compelling and your people will find it easier to understand their accountability.

It should be mentioned that simpler often means fewer. Many managers successfully ensure accountability in their group with six objectives per person, not twelve. Similarly, group or organization initiatives should be limited to three or fewer. Less is more. Beware the tendency to tack on additional objectives and projects as the year evolves rather than taking a hard look at priorities.

Practice 3—Encourage frequent communication between people whose objectives interact

To create an aligned, accountable team, you must encourage ongoing communication between your team members, extending out to other functions as required. Even high-talent A-players need an occasional prod to communicate, because they tend to be so self-sufficient. Frequent communication over the course of the year ensures that objectives and priorities are constantly reviewed. Most people depend on meetings to do this.

Understandably, meetings are the whipping boy of organizational behavior. Whatever the forum—the weekly staff meeting, program management reviews, project updates—meetings are often unfocused, inefficient, and ineffective. Patrick Lencioni, author of *Death by Meeting,*[6] does a brilliant job of articulating a formula for structuring and leading various types of meetings. Briefly, his approach requires strong leaders to maintain focus and surface controversy. It also recommends different meetings for different purposes:

1. Daily, brief standup meetings to review schedules, expedite problems, and stay aligned on tactical issues

2. Weekly meetings to focus on accountability to metrics, avoiding the distractions of impromptu problem solving

3. As-needed problem-solving meetings, bringing together the right people with the right data to make decisions

4. Quarterly strategic reviews to maintain focus on the big picture

Aside from meetings, an important way to ensure alignment within your organization is to simply touch base with your colleagues regularly and assist your people to do the same. Most busy managers report that they should spend twice as much time knocking on doors. Upper management gets frustrated with anyone who operates as a loner. They expect you to drop in periodically to your colleagues' offices to discuss progress on pressing priorities and to proactively resolve controversies. If you *get it*, you will devote time to developing professional relationships with *all* your peers, especially those with whom you conflict.

> *SPX, a high-performing industrial conglomerate, attributes part of its success to a long-standing tradition of managers "playing catch." People who are insular, including top executives, don't survive.*

Much of our time as organizational consultants is focused on helping managers adopt this practice, especially the introverts. Managers who *get it* find time to talk and listen to their staff and peers, inside and outside the conference room. They continually ask questions about other people's priorities and the degree to which their efforts are aligned.

Looking back to your signature style (Chapter 2), it is important for you to find a way to adopt all three of these practices naturally. When you do this, it will be easy and enjoyable to keep your people aligned. Even more enjoyable will be the results you see when your people stay focused on top priorities and embrace accountability as a challenge rather than something to be feared.

Reduce Uncertainty

*"I wish I knew how to handle certain parts of my job,
and I wish I could admit it to my boss."*

—90% of people in organizations, at all levels

Even if your people understand their priorities and accountability, most are more confused than they will admit. We privately hear this from people at all levels, including top management. This is especially true in matrix organizations, where lines of authority are complex, or in fast-changing organizations, where the rules of engagement are unclear.

The following chart illustrates how different types of people respond to uncertainty. The first group, the A-players, comprises 10% of the people in most groups and are unique. They thrive on uncertainty and tend to get restless, even sloppy, when working with the routine, clear-cut parts of their jobs. This group is the exception to the rule. They typically do not want more certainty and will revolt against it.

On the opposite pole, C-players typically comprise 20% of an organization. They thrive on certainty. They become disorganized, overwhelmed, and often fearful when dealing with the stress of those parts of their jobs that are uncertain to them.

The majority of people in organizations, the solid B-players, tend to handle both certainty and uncertainty fairly well; however, they can frustrate if their jobs are ill defined or they don't receive enough support from their managers.

To reduce uncertainty in your group, first follow the two steps already addressed in this chapter: upgrading talent and making sure that priorities are clarified. However, even if you have A/B-players who are crystal clear about what is expected of them, accountability will still hit speed bumps. B-players, typically 70% of your team, need continual facilitation and support. Even A-players need an occasional course correction, especially if their ego strength is off the charts. For you to *get it*, and help them *get it*, you need to make ongoing efforts to reduce the uncertainty all members of your team face.

There are some causes of uncertainty not within your control—economic cycles, customer needs, technology advances, policy shifts, matrix reporting, and performance gaps in other functions. If you, or your staff, cannot control a cause of uncertainty, at least you can open up communication on the issue. Very often, you can reduce fear and

51

	A-Players (10%)		B-Players (70%)		C-Players (20%)	
Facing Low Uncertainty	**Feel**:	Bored, restless	**Feel**:	Satisfied	**Feel**:	Secure
	Do:	Perform routinely, may be careless with routine tasks	**Do**:	Perform well consistently	**Do**:	Spend excessive time with simple tasks
Facing Moderate Uncertainty	**Feel**:	Effective, powerful	**Feel**:	Challenged	**Feel**:	Tense
	Do:	Work tenaciously	**Do**:	Perform well by working hard	**Do**:	Become disorganized, play politics, show inconsistent results
Facing High Uncertainty	**Feel**:	Excited	**Feel**:	Frustrated	**Feel**:	Fearful, demotivated
	Do:	Seek independence	**Do**:	Seek structure and feedback	**Do**:	Avoid/deny problems, show incompetence, blame others

frustration by shining a light on the shapeless form lurking in the shadows.

> *Mike was a project manager for a large construction firm. He managed a cross-functional team of people who reported directly to finance, engineering, architecture, supply chain, and operations. His largest customer had a personal relationship with Mike's manager, often bypassing the project team with change orders and unpredictable requests. After several frustrating months of trying to change the customer's behavior, Mike realized that tolerance was the only solution. He called a meeting with his team to "take the point of view of the customer" and reinforce their customer focus. The team lightened up enough to realize that the distractions were not their biggest problem.*

Although many causes of uncertainty facing your team are not directly within your control, others are. They require skill to manage. You may wish to master these fundamentals:

1. *Coach and facilitate*—Coaching is what you do one on one to help people solve isolated problems or assume projects. Facilitation is what you do daily to support your people, often spending up to 30% of your time looking for ways to reduce uncertainty among your team members. A-players need only occasional nudges. C-players may need concentrated coaching. B-players, the majority of your staff, need consistent check-ins and encouragement to knock on your door.

2. *Clarify roles and responsibilities*—Whether your organization is structured traditionally or as a matrix, I'd bet you $1000 that half your people need role clarification. Of course they won't admit it, not wanting to appear ignorant. They want *you* to raise the issue. The solution is not necessarily more detailed job descriptions. They want you to facilitate occasional conversations with their peers to sort out who is responsible for what, especially in the grey areas. Process-mapping exercises are especially powerful to clarify overlaps in responsibility and accountability.

3. *Announce more frequently*—Employees at all levels are hungry for information. If you set aside time during regular meetings to pass along news, it helps create clarity and reduce fear that comes from the rumor mill. People are particularly interested in customer news and senior management decisions, especially the *why* behind these decisions.

4. *Give feedback skillfully*—Employees are hungry for feedback, despite their apprehension about it. You would be wise to seek training in the art of giving feedback. Whether you are pulling an employee aside for a course correction or conducting an annual review, some techniques make the discussion easy and effective. The most important key is to use Socratic methods in which the EMPLOYEES do most of the talking. When they "own" the feedback, their uncertainty is minimized.

5. *Beware of brainstorming*—If you are a creative or visionary thinker, be careful when you brainstorm with your group. Your people may take your what-ifs as delegations. They probably won't tell you when they are confused, so when

53

you see a lot of heads nodding, make sure you clarify deliverables before you adjourn.

When you *get it* as a manager, you will regularly scan your team to monitor their levels of certainty and uncertainty, confidence and fear. This may be particularly difficult if you are a self-sufficient personality and expect your people to be "wired" the same way you are. This is a common trap if you are a high-potential manager or high-level executive.

I was once conducting a team-building session with a new GM and staff of a Corning division. His signature style was intense, fast-moving, and understated. His people were a little intimidated and did not know how to persuade him. I asked the group if they would like to learn his formula for "being sold an idea." They brightened and scrambled for their pens. He was delighted to go to the whiteboard and outline a six-step process while they wrote furiously. He was pleased, but also a little confused about why he needed to spell it out.

Delegate "Unreasonably"

Jillian is a hands-on manager with deep product knowledge. She works long hours, never missing deadlines. She can answer the most detailed questions from her staff, and her manager loves the fact that he can seldom stump her. She has been promoted several times because of her expertise and work ethic. Unfortunately, Jillian often does things herself rather than delegate them. She would rather complete a task quickly than take time to coach others. She believes that people should be stretched reasonably to avoid overwhelming them. Although her manager respects her ability, she is at the bottom of his succession plan and her most talented people are seeking more challenging jobs.

If Jillian better understood her team's need for challenge, she would be more willing to delegate. She would not always try to be so "reasonable" when doing so. Let's first review the basics of delegation. Consider the following diagram.

Early in your career, you achieved results by virtue of what you knew and did. Obviously, there is a limit to what you can know and do yourself. To improve results, you must substitute *asking* for knowing and *delegating* for doing. This is one reason people quip that a CEO "knows nothing and does nothing." This is only partly tongue in cheek. In a very real sense, your people should be operating more tactically than you, and you should devote significant time to facilitating their efforts.

Delegation is built on the foundation of asking questions. It's easy to underestimate the power of asking, or more precisely, of "active listening." You no doubt understand the principle. Active listening is more than keeping your mouth shut. It is an alert state of mind, actively probing the thoughts of the speaker. In fact, if you look at every critical management practice—interviewing, meeting leadership, persuasion, negotiation, performance review, delegation—active listening is the foundation.

When you delegate by listening actively, you guide employees' thinking about how to accomplish a task/project rather than do the thinking yourself. Over time, you increase employees' knowledge, hopefully to exceed your own knowledge. Ultimately, you leverage your efforts and allow your people to be accountable for the results in your department.

If you fail to listen while delegating, you risk missing critical information, giving irrelevant information, wasting time, or stifling creative thinking and initiative. By the way, if you have difficulty listening in general, you have more than *getting it* at stake. This can be fatal for your career advancement, especially if you are verbose.

Although listening is the foundation of delegation, there are other delegation techniques you'll need to master. Delegation is more than just assigning work. When done properly, delegation raises the capabilities of your staff to a new level. Below are a few simplified techniques to enhance your delegation effectiveness.

1. Be thoughtful about *what* you delegate to *whom*. Give the most complex tasks and projects to A-players to stretch them. Delegate moderately complex tasks and projects to B-players. Delegate routine tasks to C-players. If you want to develop A/B-players, they should feel *just enough* risk of failure to create emotional arousal. Adrenaline enhances memory and makes new lessons permanent.

2. Ask your staff at least annually, "What would you like to take off my plate to learn?"

3. Take time to discuss a challenging delegation. Spend more time asking questions than giving direction and advice. Brainstorm approaches. If they propose a bad idea, don't correct them immediately. Ask them to anticipate the impact of implementing their idea. Tell stories about times you handled similar situations effectively...or made great mistakes. Agree on timeframes for next steps and define decisions they can make without your input. These steps may take an hour or more but will save you time over the long run and create more empowerment.

4. For all delegations, don't just outline the project. First explain *why* you are delegating to them, including benefits to both them and the business.

5. Make sure people know how their success will be measured. Although formal metrics are not always practical for all delegations, a discussion of measurement will help both of you think more clearly about accountability.

So what about the notion of being "unreasonable"? Why would you want to do that?

Most people have a mindset that defines what is reasonable, feasible, and achievable. In a competitive business climate, this often translates to "mediocre." Excellence comes from exploding the boundaries of reason. To create a high-performing, accountable team, you must be willing to stretch people past the point they believe is reasonable. Initially, most people see this as unfair, impossible, or intimidating. Over time, they experience success and learn to exceed their own expectations. To create a team that *gets it*, your people must periodically feel an excitement that just borders on the edge of fear.

In Chapter 2, we outlined the importance of balancing ego and modesty, including using ego strength to your advantage. Your people should see your expectations as a show of your ego strength. Your show of strength should not push them to the point of terror, but dilation of the pupils and sweaty palms is a good thing—their palms, not yours. Your talented people *want* to be stretched, as long as you have the modesty to listen and provide support. Your staff gains pride and self-esteem from working with you to accomplish more than they thought possible.

Some soul searching on your part may be needed here. A prerequisite to delegate unreasonably is to convince yourself that YOU REALLY WANT TO OPERATE MORE STRATEGICALLY. If your core values dictate that you prefer hands-on work rather than delegation, you'll never be effective supervising a large group. Be honest with yourself. Take a long walk in the woods. Confer with your significant other or mentors. Your desire to play a larger game must be strong enough to overcome the discomfort you will feel when your people say, "I can't do it."

Obsess over Metrics

It's oft been said, "if you measure it, you can control it." Control is required to reduce undesirable variability in performance. As such, measurement is the foundation of performance management. Here is a more powerful quote you can put on your desk: "If your people measure it, they can hold themselves accountable." If your team is savvy with metrics, accountability becomes evident to the rest of the organization.

Whether you are using simple metrics or elaborate scorecards, the attention you pay to metrics will set the tone for your group. If you treat metrics casually, so will your people. The term "obsess" is not too extreme here. Given the distractions that vie for your people's attention, anything short of obsession can become marginalized.

Fortunately, if you follow the other fundamentals outlined above—upgrading talent, aligning priorities, reducing uncertainty, and delegating unreasonably—your obsession with metrics should not be too difficult or consuming.

I Get It!

As you might expect, there exists a simplified formula. To obsess over metrics, you must be thoughtful, frequent, focused, visual, and supportive. Let's look at these elements separately.

Be thoughtful

A few hidden dangers lurk within the world of metrics, the "dark side," in the words of Joe Wright, CEO of Master Chemical. One danger relates to politicization. Sometimes, stretch goals and public accountability encourage people to "game" the system, because of fear of punishment. Even talented people are occasionally guilty of spinning their quarterly numbers. If top executives set unachievable targets and then shame people for not reaching them, this results in misbehavior and unintended consequences such as avoidance of accountability. Thus, one goal of formulating metrics is to anticipate unproductive or unintended behavior. This highlights the importance of thoughtful design and planning.

Be frequent

How often should metrics be discussed and evaluated? It depends on whether you are talking about individual or group reviews. Individually, reviews should occur more than annually, perhaps monthly or quarterly. In fact, many experts believe that if metrics are reviewed regularly, the need for the annual review disappears. This is especially true if reviews include skilled coaching. At a staff level, most high-performing teams review metrics weekly.

Be focused

Maintaining a clear focus during staff reviews is an elusive dream for many teams. Too often, staff meetings become a disjointed discussion of problems rather than a focused review of accountability. The most effective team leaders create a review that is solely focused on metrics, similar to the Lencioni model.[6] Problem solving is reserved for other types of meetings. In addition, a skilled leader maintains focus on an established agenda, drawing out controversial issues and ensuring participation.

Be visual

The most effective performance scorecards incorporate effective visuals, if only up-down arrows and red-yellow-green codes. Pictures are often worth a thousand words, improving the efficiency of the review. Although not everyone is a visual thinker, graphics and charts offer perspective and insight. The popularity of whiteboard discussions illustrates the power of visuals. So does the concept of visual factory management,[7] which incorporates observable, real-time measures of productivity and quality. The more you can grab people's attention, the more they will be compelled by your data.

Be supportive

Fear is the enemy of accountability. Although some managers believe that a dose of fear is healthy and good for motivation, fear always creates hidden costs. Studies have consistently shown that people are more productive, engaged, and accountable when their managers are supportive. Joseph Stalin built his legacy on fear management...'nuff said. Frankly, managers who depend on fear for motivation are either lacking influence skill or playing out a sadistic need to bolster their weak self-esteem.

"Whenever there is fear, you will get wrong figures."

—J. Edwards Deming

Recap

Creating accountability within your team is a mark of *getting it* as a manager. High-performing teams want not only to achieve results but also to be held accountable. To maximize accountability, you must first recruit and develop a talented staff. Next, you must help your staff clarify their objectives, strategically as well as tactically. They must align their priorities with upper management and cross-functional peers. Once your people are pointed in the right direction, you must reduce the uncertainty that hinders them from execution. Once they are operating confidently, you can then leverage yourself by delegating more work and thinking more strategically. Finally, if you put an obsessive focus on performance metrics, accountability becomes a source of satisfaction for your staff and an inspiration for the rest of the organization.

Chapter 5

Influence Others

> **Warning Signs That You Need to Be More Influential**
> - You are sometimes puzzled by your colleagues' motives.
> - Some people seem to avoid you.
> - You are more effective with logical, calm discussions than conflict or controversy.

If you read a hundred books on the topic of influence, a pattern will hit you between the eyes. The same list of skills shows up again and again:

- "emotional intelligence," understanding others' ideas and feelings

- active listening

- relationship building

- enhancing others' self-esteem

- managing controversy skillfully

These are the fundamentals, which we will outline in this chapter with an eye toward simplicity. But we'll go a step further. In addition to learning the fundamentals, you can gain an edge that you won't get from the typical books and seminars. As in past chapters, we will help you focus on the deeper values that truly drive the motives of your peers. If you understand what your peers really want, you can tailor your approach. You don't need to be a psychologist to do this, you just need a willingness to be observant and thoughtful.

I Get It!

Understand the Real Motives of Your Colleagues

Lisa was an HR Director in a $300M division. As the organization quickly grew, the senior staff struggled with growing pains, becoming embroiled in silo thinking and finger pointing. At first Lisa tried, unsuccessfully, to improve cooperation with policies and conflict skill training. Then she tried a values-based approach. She analyzed the core values of each of her peers, using this insight to engage in one-on-one coaching behind the scenes. Lisa learned to influence each of her peers differently. One by one, Lisa was able to help her peers shift their behavior. In addition, because they were impressed with Lisa's deep understanding of them, they saw her as an ally rather than a meddler.

On the next page is a worksheet you can use to apply the values-analysis technique from Chapters 2 and 3 to one of your key colleagues. Pick someone who is most important for you to influence. As before, one of goals of this exercise is to help you develop strategies for dealing with people. Another goal is to give you practice in being more psychologically minded. The key is to focus on the person's consistent behavior patterns, using this insight to glean what he or she truly values. In the first section, start by listing your colleague's *spoken* beliefs and priorities. This will allow you to identify gaps where they he or she not be walking the talk.

Translating behavior patterns into core values is always a challenging task. Sometimes it merely takes some common sense. An illustration may help.

Tim is the quality director in a turnaround business. He was recently charged with radically redesigning the processes that link sales with operations. This included implementing a new ERP module that reengineered production scheduling. Tim frequently talked about the necessity of everyone showing courage and communicating openly to challenge bad practices. He was inspiring on the podium; however, Tim spent most of his time in his office, designing detailed plans and delegating dirty work to his staff. He refused to get involved in the conflicts that arose between sales managers, schedulers, and production supervisors. His core values, in reality, supported neither courage nor communication.

Worksheet to Brainstorm a Colleague's Core Values

List examples of your colleague's spoken beliefs and priorities, which may not reflect real core values:	
List examples of your colleague's habitual behavior, those things that he or she does repeatedly and consistently at work. This includes tasks that are most enjoyable to your colleague, and those things he or she has a reputation for doing.	Stemming from the patterns of behavior in the left column, what appear to be your colleague's underlying values?
List any emotional reactions your colleague has shown at work in the past year. These could be positive emotions or negative emotions (joy, excitement, frustration, anger, apprehension).	
List how your colleague spends most of his or her time and money at work.	

Pretend that your job is to assist Tim in his efforts. If you analyze his values, you may conclude that he is an introvert who values planning and avoiding conflict. Despite his standup skills, he is not a hands-on change leader. To influence Tim, you would never ask him to get directly involved in a controversial issue. Nor would you try to change his stripes. Rather, you would allow him to do most of the planning and fix difficult problems yourself.

In Chapter 3, we provided a few principles to help you translate your values analysis of your boss into useful tactics. Similarly, some principles can be applied to peers and other colleagues:

- Remember that you can't change anyone's core values. You need to accept their natural style, warts and all. If you are clever, you can work within the constraints of their values.

- When you sell an idea to a colleague, you must satisfy his or her underlying values, not just their stated business priorities. In most cases, your colleagues will have values that are healthy and aligned with organization values; thus, your task is to use these values to create a common ground. If your colleagues' core values are dysfunctional, however (e.g., they are self-centered or manipulative), your options will be limited.

- If a colleague has a complex set of values, this is an advantage to you. The colleague may be harder to understand, but you can appeal to him or her with a broader range of persuasive approaches. For example, let's say a colleague values perfection and confrontation to the point that he or she is overbearing. Rather than write your colleague off, you may realize that you both share the value of perfection. Armed with this knowledge, you may find ways to foster conversations, and eventually a more trusting relationship, by discussing common interests in quality or procedural details. Simply sharing common ground can make you more trusted and therefore influential.

- Once you appreciate that all your colleagues have underlying sets of values and motives, you will feel more comfortable relating to them. Rather than being wowed by their talent or frustrated by their seemingly irrational behavior, you will see them as complex and inevitably flawed—just like you and me.

Listen 'til It Stops Hurting

Listening has drawn attention from a variety of wise scholars:

> *"We have two ears and one mouth so that we can listen twice as much as we speak."*
>
> —Epictetus

> *"Courage is what it takes to stand up and speak; courage is also what it takes to sit down and listen."*
>
> —*Winston Churchill*

> *"Listen or thy tongue will keep thee deaf."*
>
> —Native American Indian Proverb

> *"No one is listening until you fart."*
>
> —Author Unknown

In your family life, the benefits of listening are clear: The quality of your relationships with significant others, whether they be spouse, children, or parents, is directly related to your listening. In your work life, the value of listening gets even more compelling. Listening is directly related to your performance, income, and promotion potential. I can tell you from personal experience as a consultant to senior management that poor listening and/or verbosity is a common cause of candidates being disqualified from consideration. You may remember from Chapter 4 and the appendix that one of the ten versatility factors is *listening*.

Consider the following management skills: interviewing, selling, negotiation, delegation, training, coaching, performance review, and conflict management. A core principle underlying all of these skills is listening. In its simplest form, listening means keeping your mouth shut and your ears open. It also means "seeking to understand" another's point of view. A skilled listener is patient, purposeful and Socratic.

I Get It!

"When questioned (a skilled listener) can answer
briefly, and when he asks (a question) he waits and
listens to the answer, which few are prepared to do."[1]

—Socrates

All of us struggle with listening from time to time. When this happens to you, what is going on? You may be filled with enthusiasm. Or you may have a brilliant point to make. Or the other person is boring you to tears. And hey, that extra cup of coffee doesn't exactly help the situation.

The challenge is even greater if you are highly intelligent, energetic, type-A driven, or a natural leader. In fact, many high-potential managers describe listening as literally painful, even those who *get* the importance of listening. Think about biting your tongue with a long-winded colleague...or being late to a meeting when one of your staff badly needs your ear...or tolerating your spouse unloading on you. While your mind is fighting to convince itself to listen, your gut is screaming to do something else.

"Active" listening is a good prescription for restlessness. One benefit of active listening is that you get to ask questions, which is more satisfying than passively standing mute. Still, asking questions requires that you spend 90% of your time in a passive mode, allowing the other person to have all the fun. There must be a better way.

Just as athletes push through pain to achieve an endorphin rush, listeners can have a similar experience. The secret is to experience the rush. If you feel pleasure, you'll keep doing whatever caused it. Not a complicated principle. This is one of the keys to basic psychology. To experience the rush, you need to see a benefit to the other person or yourself. Sometimes you have to look closely at the other person to see a benefit. For example, the other person:

- ...becomes increasingly enthused by the fact that you care about his idea. You see that you have just made his day. Deep down, you know that he will think about this moment every morning on the way to work for a month.

- ...just discovered the answer to a confusing problem, guided by your patient questions. She now feels more empowered to solve her own problems in the future. You will spend less time coaching in the future because you invested time now.

- ...realizes that you care more about him than yourself, at least for a couple minutes. You see a smile in his eyes. In the future, he is willing to go through a wall for you.

As John Cleese once said in a training video about coaching, "Think of listening as an act of generosity." Of course, generosity won't motivate you if you are a "taker" rather than a "giver" at heart. If you are self-absorbed, arrogant, or mercenary by nature, you will always put your needs above others. You will never *get it*.

So how do you become a better listener? First, read a book on the topic of active listening. You will learn techniques such as probing, clarifying, acknowledging, and summarizing. Then practice the techniques relentlessly over a period of at least 30 days, using aids such as reminder cards. Attend training in the disciplines of interviewing, negotiation, coaching, and persuasion, emphasizing the underlying skills in listening. If you *really* want to master the skills, partner with HR and teach a seminar on listening to your team. Most importantly, watch closely for the benefits others experience when you listen. If you look closely enough, you'll see their pleasure. And your pain will go away.

Elevate Self-Esteem

I once met Kathy Dannemiller, one of the best business developers in my industry. She was on a first-name basis with many of the CEOs of the Fortune 100. When I asked her about her secret to success, she gave me a million-dollar smile and said, "It's simple. People like who they are when they're with me!"

She is quotable, indeed. But what does it mean when a manager "likes who he is"? Kathy was certainly not talking about a touchy-feely therapy exercise. She was talking about self-esteem.

What is self-esteem in the context of business? Simply put, self-esteem is a state of mind in which a person believes that he or she is worthy. This state of mind is linked to feelings. When self-esteem is high, a person feels confident and good. Absent are feelings of self-doubt or fear of judgment by others. There is no anxiety or apprehension. Thinking is clear, decisiveness is high, and action comes easily. People with extraordinarily high self-esteem describe a state of high-energy peacefulness, almost euphoria.[2] This doesn't mean they are passive. In fact, some of the most driven, competitive CEOs describe the same experience.

Some people have naturally high self-esteem. The extent to which self-esteem is genetically programmed or learned from early family experience is still a debate. I've interviewed successful executives from a broad range of backgrounds. Some were privileged, and others had dysfunctional families or tragic early experiences. Interestingly, executives with high self-esteem come from both camps. Clearly, there is a genetic component.

Although self-esteem is naturally high in some people, it can be raised or lowered by day-to-day events, including interactions with you. This is especially true of people whose natural self-esteem is in the low to moderate range. This is a great opportunity for you as a manager who seeks to master the art of influence. When you raise others' self-esteem, they attribute their positive thoughts and feelings to you. They are more likely to listen to you and assume that you are trustworthy.

Sadly, some managers do not believe that self-esteem is important. It blows me away when I see managers, especially top executives, intentionally generate fear in their people to motivate them. Fear creates short-term activity but never truly motivates. People want to be supported and respected. In Chapter 4 we concluded that when your people feel supported, they are more motivated to be accountable. In the same way, when your colleagues' self-esteem is high, they are more motivated to listen to you. Again, the theme emerges that fear is the enemy.

So what are the best ways to raise self-esteem in your colleagues? Here are some techniques. I advise you to pick one a week and immerse yourself completely in it.

1. First, do some soul searching to "admit what your colleagues already know about you," as outlined in Chapter 2. If you have a lifelong habit of diminishing others' self-esteem, it is likely that you value and actually enjoy doing this. A professional coach or counselor may be required for you to decide whether you really want to change.

2. If you have a history of compromising people's self-esteem, it can take a long time to recover your reputation. For example, if you have harshly criticized people, they will continue to raise their defensive guards in your presence. Or if you have been impatient, your colleagues may have concluded that you don't really care about their ideas. They may even believe that you don't like them as people! The good news is that the more positive feelings you create, the

quicker a person will forget the old memories. This is because memories are amplified by emotions. Even though you may have created deep negative memories from your past behavior, if you consistently create emotionally positive feelings, your efforts will pay off.

3. Identify colleagues whose self-esteem is naturally low. These are typically thin-skinned people who are easily intimidated. They become defensive when criticized. They visibly brighten when you listen or pay them compliments. With these people, you need a communication strategy. Make notes about what they value and what motivates them. Consider the specific things you could do or say that could raise their self-esteem. Then simply follow your strategy, much as a star salesperson would follow a strategy for key prospects.

4. Notice that raising others' self-esteem does not require you to be "too nice" or less assertive. In fact, there is no reason to compromise your outspokenness or standards. What is important is *how* you deliver a message. For example, if you want to assert yourself with a colleague who is not meeting a commitment, the statement "You're incompetent and a waste of good oxygen" does not exactly raise self-esteem. It is more effective to say, "Sam, I'm in a spot because I haven't received the financial statements from you. What can I do to help you complete them today?"

5. Be willing to apologize. First, if you want to transform a relationship with a colleague whom you have intimidated, apologize for your past behavior. Then as you go forward, be willing to admit your contribution (or your staff's contribution) to problems. Review the section Balance Ego and Modesty in Chapter 2. Remember that when you show modesty or vulnerability, most people experience an increase in their self-esteem. This is not because they perceive you as weak, but because they perceive you as an equal.

6. Last but not least, LISTEN. When you listen, you show respect. People love to be shown even a tiny amount of consideration. Often, listening takes time. It is almost always well spent.

I Get It!

> *Daren, a type-A executive in a fast-growing division was giving me a plant tour. I noticed that during the tour, Daren "looked through" everyone we met. No smiles or hellos. He was not an abusive leader but simply valued efficiency. I later discovered that many people felt intimidated by him. The organization culture was self-conscious and mistake-avoidant, reflecting people's fear. Daren was shocked and embarrassed when I gave him feedback. He truly wanted to be a "good guy" and effective leader. Over the next few years, Daren made efforts to raise others' self-esteem. He saw it as a strategic challenge for him and the business. He didn't lose his power. In fact, his people's respect for him increased exponentially. He was much more influential.*

Develop Trusting Relationships

On the surface, relationship building would seem to be a simple skill that 90% of managers have already mastered. Only obnoxious, antisocial people don't build relationships. Right? Not exactly.

If you study the best influencers in business, whether salespeople or CEOs, you'll discover that they know a secret. That is, relationships are more than cordial acquaintances between people who have something in common. Relationships are based on trust. Trust occurs between you and your colleagues under the following conditions:

1. You share common goals; personal agendas are secondary.

2. Your expectations of each other are not just met but are exceeded.

3. There is lack of fear of either personal pain or business pain.

4. You both value straight talk.

Let's look at these conditions, one at a time.

Condition 1—You share common goals; personal agendas are secondary.

Throughout history, shared goals have created political, religious, and social alliances. It is human nature to trust people who share the same purpose. Tragically, the converse is often true, as in politically and religiously-fueled war. In the business world, alliances and wars exist on a smaller scale. It is easier to trust people who are striving, sometimes fighting, for the same goals.

Even when colleagues share common goals, personal agendas can get in the way. A common example is when both sales managers and quality managers want to satisfy the customer but their functional priorities make cooperation difficult. Sales managers are rewarded for volume, whereas quality managers are rewarded for eliminating defects. As such, functional priorities can hinder a common agenda. Similarly, individual people can hold personal agendas, for example, when an ambitious manager resists giving credit to colleagues in order to feather his own nest.

Obviously, your first task is to evaluate your own personal agendas to see if they conflict with organizational goals, group goals, or your colleagues' goals. You can't create trusting relationships if others believe that you are on your own program. Your next task is to evaluate the personal agendas of others. Although you many not have full control over people who have self-serving agendas, you may be able to help them see what their agendas cost them and the group.

If you are lucky, your organization and your manager *get it,* making efforts to align goals and priorities (Chapter 4). This helps create shared goals between you and your colleagues. If your organization does not have aligned priorities, you will have to make extraordinary efforts to create a common ground with the people you must influence. This will require you to become skilled at all the fundamentals outlined in this chapter.

Condition 2—Your expectations of each other are not just met but exceeded.

On an obvious level, trust comes when people follow through. Your colleagues trust you when you do what you promise, and vice versa. If you have problems meeting your commitments, even "trivial" infractions such as being late to meetings or occasionally missing a deadline, trust is compromised.

Apart from just meeting colleagues' expectations, *getting it* requires that you exceed them. When you do this, you impress people. More importantly, you create an emotional bond. Just as a family relationship has an emotional foundation, so does a true business relationship. Of course, the emotional bond is very different in these two types of relationships, but the bond serves the same purpose—establishing a deeper level of trust and kinship.

Richard Abraham, in his delightful book, *Mr. Shmooze,*[3] outlines how world-class influencers operate in business. Their secret is more than doing favors such as giving away baseball tickets. There are more subtle strategies, such as:

- Watching and listening carefully for what colleagues truly value.

- Focusing on benefits to others, especially financial benefits.

Something magical happens when you show a colleague that you are willing to go beyond meeting his or her expectations. When you show a colleague that you really care about him or her, even in a trivial way such as asking about the family photo on the desk, your colleague feels a deeper bond of trust.

> *I once wanted to thank a client, Don, for his sponsorship of our consulting firm over many years. Although a gift would not be appropriate, I wanted something symbolic of my appreciation, so I confidentially asked several members of his staff about his hobbies, interests, and passions. I discovered that he was an ardent fan of the Seinfeld TV show. I researched and found an autographed photo of the "Soup Nazi" character, with a handwritten scrawl by the actor, "Don...no soup for you!" It was a little corny, but it earned a smile and a place on his credenza. What better way to show trust than being willing to be lighthearted and a little corny?*

Condition 3—There is lack of fear of either personal pain or business pain.

This condition is straightforward. If you believe that people will hurt you or the business, you won't trust them. Conversely, if people believe that you are capable of inflicting pain, they won't trust you and will avoid you.

Regarding personal pain, people's actions can lower another's self-esteem, by providing hurtful criticism or clumsy remarks, for example. Other forms of hurt include public humiliation, exclusion of people from meetings, or unfair personnel decisions. When people are hurt, they naturally fear being hurt again. They no longer trust.

On the business side, pain occurs when a bad decision has a negative impact on execution, customer satisfaction, or financial performance. Pain often results from incompetent people who don't perform. It is hard to trust anyone who hurts the business.

Your task is to make sure that you don't create pain. You need to master the art of elevating others' self-esteem. You also need to ensure that your decisions and performance create value for the business. More importantly, you need to make sure that everyone under your leadership does the same.

Condition 4—You both value straight talk.

> *"Candor and trust are king in building a competitive and efficient workplace."*

—Jack Welch, former Chairman, GE

Interestingly, Welch pairs candor with trust. In a very real sense, candor builds trust when you show people that you trust them enough to be honest. Techniques in conflict management include the use of straight talk, especially when you are addressing a colleague with whom trust is already low.

If you have ever been accused of being "too nice" or conflict avoidant, you may suffer the illusion that friendliness creates trust. In reality, if friendliness is not balanced by assertiveness, you build a "wall of civility" around you. This makes it difficult for others to know you deeply or trust you.

For people to know you deeply, they must know your thoughts and feelings. Let's discuss thoughts first. If your natural personality is introverted or extremely understated, your colleagues may not know your thoughts on critical issues that affect them. Because Homo sapiens evolved over tens of thousands of years with an oral tradition, most people have a deep need for verbal intimacy.

I once knew a director of engineering who was a minimalist verbally. He was brilliant strategically and impressive when making client presentations. With peers, however, he didn't socialize much. Nor did he feel the need to stop by their offices for occasional chats. In fact, sometimes he was so deep in thought that he didn't even say hello in the hallways. Because he was a self-sufficient personality, he assumed that others were "wired" the same way. His colleagues didn't trust him until he made conscious efforts to reach out.

Expressing feelings is just as important as expressing thoughts. As such, straight talk also requires "straight feelings." This is tricky in the business world because some feelings are inappropriate to express, such as outbursts and tantrums. Some feelings are both appropriate and effective, however. Expression of such feelings can be subtle, such as a twinkle in the eye or a slight frown. Think about the most trustworthy people you know. Generally, these are people who have a quick smile and maybe a hearty laugh. They are easy to read; for example, when they get frustrated, their faces show it. They express themselves appropriately, avoiding rage or emotional drama. Simply put, they are open.

If you are naturally a low-key personality, all you may need to do is crank it up a notch. Going back to the theme of a signature style (Chapter 2), if you express yourself in a natural way, even with subtle words and expressions, you create a level of intimacy that leads to trust.

> *"Experience teaches us that silence terrifies people the most."*
>
> —Bob Dylan

Generate Controversy to Gain Respect

Any CEO will tell you that one of the most respectable traits of high-performing managers is fearlessly attacking controversial problems. In fact, the bigger the problem and more controversy involved, the better. Because CEOs tend to be fearless themselves, by nature and because of their position, they assume that everyone else should be the same. They disrespect anyone who isn't. They secretly judge anyone who is insecure or uptight about political correctness.

> *"Being responsible sometimes means pissing people off....Trying to get everyone to like you is a sign of mediocrity. Ironically, you'll simply ensure that the*

*only people you'll wind up angering are the most
creative and productive people in the organization."*

—Former Secretary of State Gen. Colin Powell

In our experience as executive assessors, somewhere between 10% and 15% of mid-upper–level managers embrace controversy. They tend to be naturally thick-skinned, courageous and enjoy the thrill of a healthy conflict. Sometimes their social skills are rough, and many will articulate the need to develop finesse. But these are the people who don't hesitate to walk into someone's office, even two levels above them, and say, "Hey, do you have a minute? Something is bugging me...." Even though they can ruffle feathers, they tend get picked for the best assignments. Other things equal, they tend to get promoted first.

Some great examples of generating controversy:

- An operations manager speaks out in a staff meeting when he feels that salespeople spin their forecasts.

- An HR director sits down in a VP's office, closing the door, to have a conversation about the VP's public criticism of HR.

- A procurement manager requires certification of a legacy supplier that has a personal history with the VP.

- A VP of sales shows courage by admitting to the senior team that the sales staff need upgrading.

- The general manager's assistant confronts her boss, politely and firmly, about unprofessional use of profanity.

- A child confronts her parents when they do the opposite of what they preach.

If you are naturally gifted with a love of controversy, please skip to the next chapter. If, however, you are among the 85–90% of people who don't enjoy generating controversy, read on. There are ways to become more proactive and assertive, and hopefully, these ways will become part of your signature style. Listed below are proven pointers. Not all of them may work for you, so you'll need to experiment.

1. Accept the fact...no, enjoy the fact...that you will compete and conflict with other ambitious peers. Like death and taxes, it is inevitable.

2. Realize that whenever you address controversy, you will not feel calm and relaxed. There is always apprehension when you create risk, triggering an innate fight-or-flight response. The greater the risk you take, the greater the reflex to fight or flee. With practice, you can learn to perceive this reflex as simply emotional arousal without the fear attached. Skilled negotiators, for example, train themselves to interpret their fear as excitement.

3. Seek out courageous colleagues who enjoy generating controversy. You don't have to change your friends, but expand your lunch partners to include people who energize and encourage you.

4. Find a mentor/protector...or two or three.

5. Know that if you change your stripes, some acquaintances will try to pull you back to a more familiar way of operating. Most people don't like change. Your "friends" may be threatened by your newfound style.

6. Collect data before you generate controversy. Be financially grounded. If you have facts and numbers to support your idea, your courage will be enhanced. You will be more credible and influential.

7. Attend training in negotiation and conflict management. Then if you *really* want to master these skills, partner with HR to teach the courses yourself.

8. You may not need to change your style completely, as emphasized in Chapter 2. Sometimes you simply need to convince yourself that the controversy is truly important to you. In other words, do what you believe in, and crank up the heat a couple of degrees.

"You gain strength, courage, and confidence by every experience in which you really stop to look fear in the face. You must do the thing which you think you cannot do."

—Eleanor Roosevelt

Recap

To be most influential with your colleagues, you first need to understand what makes them tick. Using values analysis, you may be able to determine their motives and what they expect from you. It is also important for you to master the art of active listening, even if you are a restless soul and find the process painful. By using active listening, along with other techniques, you can elevate the self-esteem of your colleagues and develop more-trusting relationships. When your colleagues see you as receptive, supportive, and trustworthy, you will be much more influential. Finally, when you become skilled at addressing controversial issues proactively and confidently, your colleagues will be even more compelled by you.

Chapter 6

Develop Business Acumen

> **Warning Signs That You Need to Develop Business Acumen**
>
> - Upper management's decisions don't make sense to you.
> - Customers' demands annoy you.
> - You feel inadequate when peers refer to financial concepts as obvious truths.

The term "acumen" is synonymous with insight, wisdom, intelligence, and shrewdness. Obviously, good business acumen takes time to develop. Early in your career, you focused on developing technical shrewdness, not business acumen. Over the years, your focus likely expanded from technical to functional to cross-functional. Depending on your current career stage, you may still need to expand your knowledge beyond your core expertise. For example you may need to learn more about operations, accounting, or product development. This is normal and good; however, most of this focus is internal to the business. Although it is important to learn internal functions and processes, ultimately, business acumen requires you to be externally focused.

> *"Inside there are only costs.*
> *Results are only on the outside."*
>
> —Peter Drucker

Ram Charan, business consultant, author, and speaker, defines business acumen as "linking an insightful assessment of the external business landscape with the keen awareness of how money can be made—and then executing the strategy to deliver the desired results."[1] Note the key themes here: markets...profit...strategy...focusing primarily on outside factors.

Business acumen is equally important to the VP, the director, and the middle manager. Even if you are mid career, you must devote a good portion of your focus outward, beyond the boundaries of your position, department, and company. *Getting it* requires that you devote significant time to developing business acumen.

Get Strategy

This section is not about strategic planning. It's about developing a strategic mindset. The quicker you understand and embrace the preoccupations of the strategic leaders in your organization, the quicker you will *get it*. "Preoccupation" is not too strong a term here, nor is "obsession." When a strategic executive stares out the window, most of the time, he or she is not thinking about the tactical details of today's problems but about strategic challenges such as value creation, future products, competition, asset restructuring, or talent acquisition.

If you are in a tactical job, it is appropriate for you to spend most of your time with tactics. But you should spend more than a tiny percentage of your time thinking strategically: you should exceed perhaps 5% as a manager, 10% as a director, and 20% as a VP. This doesn't mean that you should rush out to set up an off-site meeting. Although meetings and discussions are important, more important is how YOU think on an ongoing basis.

Consider the many ways you can become more strategically engaged:

- Brainstorm a contentious customer viewpoint during your "windshield time."

- Re-sort your priorities every morning, favoring those with strategic or value-added impact.

- Listen strategically in staff meetings, asking context questions when meetings bog down in tactical details.

- Coach a direct report on the business implications of a blunder (either their blunder or your blunder!).

- Stop by your manager's office periodically to float a big idea.

- Remember to generate "what-ifs" when you make decisions.

You get the idea.

Shifting to a broader, more strategic mode of thinking is not easy to switch on overnight, especially if your supervisor or organization keeps you tactically focused. The good news is that, over time, you can train yourself to improve your strategic acumen. Below is a list of further suggestions that can speed your progress. Make a commitment to apply a different one every month, then develop some of your own.

- Read what your boss and your boss's boss read. Ask them! Read a new book on strategy once a quarter, both classics and new best sellers.

- Subscribe to a condensed book service to expand your mindset during commutes.

- Review the sections in Chapter 3 on flying at 30,000 feet and articulating a defensible point of view. Always be ready with a couple of compelling sound bites to show senior management what you've been thinking about. Condition them to expect interesting ideas from you.

- If a senior executive ever invites you for a strategic discussion, relax. You don't exactly want to put your feet on his or her desk, but you should lighten up and enjoy yourself. Strategic executives LOVE to talk about new insights that create value for the business. Most CEOs go nuts when a week passes and no one shows the courage to stop by to challenge their thinking.

- Study your company's public documents such as annual reports, press releases, sales literature, and any information that promotes the value proposition of your business.

- During meetings, divide your notes into two columns. Write details, tactics, and actions in one column and paint a broader picture in the other column. If you are a visual thinker, draw diagrams, relationships, and trend lines.

- Master the arts of active listening and Socratic coaching. When you focus on being receptive rather than directive, your mind expands to a bigger picture.

Once you *get* strategy as a mindset rather than a discrete event, your ability to *get it* increases dramatically.

Embrace Customer and Shareholder Reality

The term "customer focus" is long-honored. There are likely few people in your organization who don't understand basic customer needs. Both external and internal customers have specific requirements for delivery, quality, communication, and budget. If you have established a reputation for exceeding the expectations of customers, I guarantee that you are on the radar screens of senior executives who are concerned with succession planning.

Although most managers *get* the importance of customers, few spend much time thinking about shareholders. Shareholder needs are not hard to understand: investors, owners, or strategic partners are primarily looking for a financial return on their investments.

Simply, an organization's highest purpose is to exceed customer and shareholder expectations. This includes helping to shape these expectations to create an advantage for your organization. To help your organization exceed expectations, you must think beyond mere stated expectations to embrace their broader realities. The reality of a customer's or shareholder's world includes

- Their unstated needs.

- Their long-term strategic challenges, such as product commoditization or globalization.

- Creating value in a way that has not yet been conceived.

- Conflicts of interest with their customers and suppliers.

- Financial realities such as required growth, available capital, debt, and margins.

- Competition within their own industry.

The point is to embrace their reality from THEIR point of view. It isn't enough for you to simply conduct market analysis, mine data, or review their RFQs (Request for Quote). If you truly have acumen and *get* the reality of customers and shareholders, you will see the world through their eyes. This includes their perceptions of *your* organization.

> *"We've been inside-out for over a hundred years.*
> *Forcing everything around the outside-in view will*
> *change the game."*

—Jack Welch, former Chairman, GE

Ultimately, the outside-in view comes from getting so close to the customer or shareholder that you see, touch, and smell what they do. In other words, you must form close relationships. Steve Yastrow, author of *Brand Harmony* and *We: The Ideal Customer Relationship*, has done a beautiful job of articulating the methods and benefits of customer-centered relationships. In *We*, he says

> *"Customers have more product and service choices than ever before, making it very difficult for them to distinguish your business solely on the merit of your product and service offerings. What can differentiate your business in the minds of customers, however, is the relationship the customer has with you."*[2]

It is easy to develop relationships with customers or shareholders if your role is business development, marketing, or product development. Relationships typically require face-to-face socializing. But what if you are an accounting or production manager? How can you meet with outsiders? Often, all you need to do is ask. If you embrace the theme of Chapter 3 of this book, you know the importance of exceeding your manager's expectations. This often requires stretching yourself outside the constraints of your role, asking for forgiveness rather than permission. You may not be given travel time and budget, but you may be creative enough to

- Get invited to a financial review for your company's shareholders.

- Conduct customer tours of your facilities.

- Volunteer to participate in a supplier quality audit.

- Attend quoting meetings, sales updates, or change-order reviews.

- Ask a top salesperson to lunch to discuss customer perspectives.

- Attend a nearby stockholder meeting.

Even if you cannot develop personal relationships with customers and shareholders, remember that embracing their reality is a mindset. It requires that you first understand their needs, then consider these needs when making decisions. If your decisions are always colored by the imperative of exceeding outsider's expectations, your business acumen will quickly become apparent to others.

Become Financially Astute

> *"Rule #1: Never lose money.*
> *Rule #2: Never forget rule #1."*

—Warren Buffett

Finance is the language of business. It's the lens that focuses priorities and the filter that defines results. Most managers see finance as a technical discipline to be learned sometime before promotion to VP. In reality, financial acumen is much more fundamental. It requires developing a mindset, just as strategic and customer-shareholder acumen does. Managers who *get it* develop financial acumen that eventually becomes intuitive. The sooner you do this, the better. Even if you spend only an hour a month, it will not take long for you to exceed the financial acumen of most top managers.

It may be helpful to visualize three levels of financial acumen, progressing from technical to intuitive:

1. Technical—competence in accounting and financial analysis

2. Decisional—understanding how financial analysis is applied to decisions, including the complex interactions between financial metrics and nonfinancial factors (politics, stakeholder bias)

3. Intuitive—always thinking in financial terms, reading between the lines of financial statements, seeing unapparent problems and opportunities, looking for ways to create value in your business

Let's look at these levels in more detail, one at a time.

Level 1—Technical

Education in accounting and finance teaches the technical and regulatory underpinnings of GAAP (Generally Accepted Accounting Principles), budgeting, cost accounting, financial statements, cash flow, financial planning, leveraging financial resources, capital allocation, and debt management. A basic technical understanding helps you measure performance and make decisions. Even if your role is in operations, sales, or HR, many of these technical finance skills are required.

There are several ways to improve your technical knowledge:

- Take a Finance for Nonfinancial Managers course as early in your career as possible, either at a local university or online.

- Read a good book on the topic.[3]

- After some study, ask your controller or friend in accounting to discuss how the basics apply to your business, perhaps over a series of lunches. You buy.

- Sponsor financial simulation training at work for your colleagues. Search the internet with the keywords "finance nonfinancial managers simulation".

Most financial statements are not complex if you understand the components. They merely restate numbers and variance. Similarly, budgets are generally straightforward, outlining detailed goals for revenue and spending. Understanding basic accounting principles and cash flow is the first step in becoming financially astute. The next step is using analysis to make decisions and understand how financial metrics interact in unapparent ways.

Level 2—Decisional

> *"Financial analysis is worthless if it isn't used to make decisions."*
>
> —Jim Cates, VP/GM, ATK Integrated Weapon Systems

I Get It!

Financial analysis drives decisions. For example, if your Return on Investment (ROI), Return on Assets (ROA), or Return on Equity (ROE) is decreasing, you evaluate the root causes and make decisions to fix them. Or, if cash generation is increasing, you may decide to invest in R&D or new equipment. The senior team and board of directors regularly evaluate complete financial statements to monitor a business's performance, with each component of the analysis potentially leading to a new decision.

Typically, decisions are guided by strategy. For instance, if an organization's mission is to "provide the highest-quality product at the lowest cost," decisions are colored by product quality, pricing, and cost. Similarly, strategies for improving manufacturing efficiency, growing top line, or reducing debt will color the decisions that are made during financial reviews. Sometimes decisions are straightforward; other times they are subjects of debate. Here are further examples of typical decisions stemming from financial analysis that are debated in organizations:

- Should increased scrap lead to an investment in new inventory control systems, upgraded machinery, or LEAN training?

- Does a decrease in sales mean we should upgrade current sales staff, add new sales positions, and/or change the marketing strategy?

- Should an increase in operating costs lead us to initiate a thorough review of material/labor/inventory, or simply initiate a price increase?

- If there is a top-line surge during an economic recovery, should we invest in a new production facility in China, push extra cash into sales/marketing efforts, or increase inventory?

As you are offered increasingly demanding assignments in your career, you will be required to make increasingly complex financial decisions. Learning to make astute decisions comes from experience and the counsel of talented mentors. If you seek mentors with strong financial acumen, your success will be greatly enhanced.

Financial analysis gets more complex and interesting when you look at interactions between the numbers and other business realities, for example, when people's biases and political agendas come into play.

You may have had an experience early in your career, managing your spending budget, focusing closely on costs. You learned that meeting your budget is a fundamental rule. Over time, you are surprised to learn that discretionary funds magically appear for projects favored by top management. A budget is not always a budget. Similarly, a profit is not always a profit, for example, when a low ROA may be deemed acceptable for a new product line that opens up a promising distribution channel. Metrics are seldom one-dimensional.

> *"Low profit is like high cholesterol. It's not the*
> *complete picture of a company's health."*

—Dave Dailey, former CEO, Florence Corporation

Below are a few more examples, based on the fictitious company Acme Products, showing how interactions can be more relevant than the numbers themselves.

- Although Acme's largest customer was sending stable orders, Acme's CEO had a gut feel that the customer would seek additional suppliers to lower costs. He asked the VP of sales and CFO to conduct a new competitive analysis, although he couldn't fully justify his request. Although the analysis was inconclusive, the CEO decided to revise the budget to require a 3% reduction in material cost and 6% increase in production efficiency. He allowed intuition to affect his financial strategy.

- In advance of annual budgeting, Acme's CEO knew that his people tended to "underspend on opportunities and overspend on habits." So he asked his managers to re-justify all budget items that carried over from the previous year. He then asked each person to propose a creative way to spend a hypothetical $50,000. Three new initiatives were funded the next year from cost savings alone.

- During a bad month, Acme's CEO scrutinized each line item of the budget, frustrating his staff, who criticized his short-term focus and micromanagement. He reminded them that an annual budget is an estimate, not an entitlement to spend, and that executives with business acumen will question their budget every day.

- After three years of 20% annual sales increases, Acme's CEO pointed out to the team that spending momentum was building. The team had quickly forgotten the pain of the last recession and had forgotten the benefits of zero-based budgeting.

- Because of their debt load and need for working capital, Acme's parent corporation tended to micromanage whenever Acme's cash flow decreased. Because the corporate office was cash-hungry in both up and down economies, Acme's management had to adjust to constantly shifting priorities and create appropriate incentives for themselves.

- When Acme was privately owned, the senior team was frustrated by the personal and often irrational agendas of owners that did not conform to sensible business practices. At one point, the owners got cold feet at the last minute on an almost-completed acquisition. The CEO first had to apologize to Acme's acquisition team and suppliers, then was forced to restructure the business. Financial metrics were changed several times that year.

- The supply chain manager wanted to contract a new supplier in Bejing. Acme required that suppliers provide specific financial statements with metrics not easily calculated by or relevant to the supplier. The contract was delayed by six months at an estimated cost of $1.3M.

- The HR manager was proud of her below-budget performance, a key metric on her performance scorecard. She was then puzzled when her VP promoted other people for "taking risks and creating business value," even when they consistently ran over budget.

"Financial analysis is more like squeezing Jello$^{®}$ than juggling balls."

—Jim Babiasz, VP Finance, Fisher & Company

Financial decisions are not always convoluted. They are typically constrained by reasonable boundaries, including GAAP and auditing practices. While budgets and metrics can be changed easily, financial reporting must be justified and conform to regulatory guidelines. Even within these constraints, however, there is plenty of wiggle room.

To make savvy financial decisions, you need to broaden your mindset to embrace the cultural, political, and economic realities of your world. Of course, this takes time. It also requires you to develop a keen interest in doing so. As we discussed in Chapter 2, only if you value it will you do it.

Listed below are some suggestions to improve your knowledge of financial decisions and the twists that make them interesting.

- Gain exposure to financial decisions. Ask to attend meetings where financials are reviewed. Look around the organization and try to figure out where money is spent and why.

- Seek a financially savvy mentor. Ask him or her interesting questions such as "What frustrates you the most about our financials?" or "Tell me about exceptions that are made to the budget and why." or "How do you conform to budget guidelines while responding to changing priorities?"

- Ask cost accountants to explain how cost systems work. Probe how process improvements on the floor impact financial statements, not just headcount and spending. Learn to see scrap, for example, as a cost trend, not just pieces and part numbers. Focus on changes over time, not just static metrics.

- Talk to your supervisor about cases when past board decisions have impacted financial priorities.

- Most of all, be patient. It takes time and experience to learn the nuances of financial interactions.

Level 3—Intuitive

I once talked to a savvy CEO and his HR VP about a hiring spec for a group-level executive. Aside from the usual financial and strategic skills, they emphasized the importance of "reading between lines." When I asked them what this meant, they elaborated, saying that it was

- the ability to look beyond performance metrics, both financial and operational, to infer the health of all areas of the business.

- *knowing* top priorities after a quick glance at the financials.

- seeing problems and opportunities that are not readily apparent from the line items.

They were seeking to hire someone with the highest level of financial acumen, that is, someone with almost psychic insight into the core drivers and future opportunities of the business. Not surprisingly, they were also looking for a successor to the CEO.

Another aspect of intuitive financial acumen relates to values that reside deep within an individual and very often operate unconsciously. One value relates to profit. Executives who *get it* view the world through profit-colored glasses. Another example is frugality. Greed and inefficiency have no place in a high-performing organization.

> *Bob Spath, a friend who has run several successful companies, tells a story of being hired to turn around a privately held company that was bleeding cash. Preparing for his first customer road trip, he was handed first-class air tickets. He quickly refused them, telling the owner, "you don't get it." He established a policy of using the cheapest flights and motels. Perks for upper management were dismantled.*

Lower costs were one key to Bob's successful turnaround, but more important was the frugal mindset he drove down into the organization. Over time, employees at all levels started to value this principle behind the financial metrics. They felt ownership for the company's success without having to think about it.

Not everyone achieves intuitive financial acumen. You need the right capabilities and values, such as conceptual skill and a keen interest in playing the game of business. You also need to devote time and do the necessary work:

- Seek exposure to the right job assignments and mentors.

- Master the technical and decisional aspects of finance.

- Take initiative to pursue learning for yourself that your organization may not provide.

- Embrace your mistakes and learn from them.

If you do the work, take the risks, and find ways to enjoy yourself in the process, your financial intuition will naturally increase. And I'll bet that someone in a corner office will enjoy watching you *get it*.

Recap

Business acumen goes beyond strategic planning, customer understanding, and financial analysis. It ultimately requires the development of a mindset. A strategic mindset means that you spend a significant portion of your time thinking about the big-picture issues facing the business, today and tomorrow. This comes from reading, listening, and brainstorming with strategic thinkers around you. A customer-shareholder mindset means that you see the world from their point of view and make ongoing efforts to shape and/or exceed their expectations. This can be accomplished with research as well as direct customer exposure. A financial mindset means first learning technical analysis and financial decision-making, then evolving to a point that you see all decisions in financial terms, intuitively.

Appendix — Versatility Worksheet

For each of the ten traits, check the *Important* column if it is important for this person's position, in light of upcoming challenges. Then in the *OK* column, check if the person is sufficiently skilled. Finally, count the number of traits where *Important* is checked but *OK* is not.

If someone is skilled on *all* important traits, his or her versatility is *High*. If the person lacks skill on *even one* important trait, you may rate his or her versatility as *Low* **if** that trait is critical to performance. If you can't clearly choose between *High* and *Low*, consider the person as *Moderate*. In general, low-versatility employees are best suited for low-change, familiar positions. Moderate-versatility employees may be limited, or may not. They should be stretched gradually to evaluate their capabilities. High-versatility employees can be given risky, challenging assignments.

Intellectual Versatility		Important	OK
Conceptual Thinking	Thinks abstractly to grasp complex, multidimensional problems. Not black-and-white. Tolerates ambiguity.		
Mental Focus	Maintains mental focus through a long conversation or a long project. Prioritizes effectively.		
Detail Versatility	Thinks at an appropriate level of detail, either macro or micro. Can go from 30,000 feet to 1,000 feet, and vice versa, "at will."		
Decisiveness/ Drive	Takes risks. Is decisive without overanalyzing or hesitating. Shows healthy impatience and urgency.		
Social Versatility			
Social Insight	Reads the points of view and feelings of others, including his or her own impact on others. Has "emotional intelligence."		
Confidence-Modesty Balance	Shows strength in BOTH areas: • Confidence—Addresses challenging tasks or people without hesitation. • Modesty—Self-effaces, maintains others' self-esteem (no arrogance).		

I Get It!

Listening	Patiently puts own agenda aside to embrace another's. Asks questions. Seeks to understand.		
Leadership Versatility			
Integrity	Values candor. Admits mistakes. Respects compliance and regulatory requirements. Acts professionally.		
Delegation	Willing to give up control. Empowers people with responsibility and authority. Leverages own efforts through others.		
Accountability	Holds people accountable to their commitments. Values results more than getting people's approval.		
	OVERALL VERSATILITY (Low, Moderate, High)		

Notes

Chapter 1

1. Collins, Jim. *Good to Great: Why Some Companies Make the Leap...and Others Don't*. Collins Business, 2001.

2. Copernicus. *De Revolutionibus Orbium Coelestium*, Book 1, Chapter 10. Easton Press, 1999.

3. Honderich, Ted. *Oxford Companion to Philosophy*. Oxford University Press, 1995.

4. Man, John. *Genghis Khan: Life, Death, and Resurrection*. St. Martin's Griffin, 2007.

5. Greenspan, Alan. *Banco de Mexico's 80th Anniversary International Conference*. Mexico City, November 14, 2005.

6. Kahaner, Larry, and Greenspan, Alan. *The Quotations of Alan Greenspan: Words from the Man Who Could Shake the World*. Adams Media Corporation, 2000.

7. Dailey, Kenneth. *The Lean Manufacturing Pocket Handbook*. DW Publishing, 2003.

8. Heller, Robert and Hindle, Tim. *Essential Manager's Manual*. DK Publishing, 1998.

Chapter 2

1. Pease, Allan and Pease, Barbara. *The Definitive Book of Body Language*. Bantam Dell, 2006.

2. Witmer, Neil, Grip, Jeff, and Sherwood, Steve. *Three Strategies Used by Extraordinary Performers*. Witmer & Associates' white paper, 2006.

3. Sherwood, Steven. *Finding Freedom: The Five Choices That Will Change Your Life*. Cincinnati Book Publishers, 2007.

Notes

4. Tolle, Eckert. *The Power of Now*. New World Library, 2004.

5. Collins, Jim. *Good to Great: Why Some Companies Make the Leap...and Others Don't*. Collins Business, 2001.

6. See lifesuccessseminars.com, outwardbound.org, and landmarkeducation.com.

Chapter 3

1. Bryant, Adam. "Think 'We' for Best Results." *New York Times*, April 18, 2009.

2. Witmer, Neil. *The Misunderstood Values of the CEO*. Unpublished technical report, 1995.

3. Grip, Jeffrey. Unpublished study, 2007.

4. Randle, Christina. *Getting It Together: Gaining the Thriving Professional's Effective EDGE*. Cornerstone, 2007.

5. Allen, David. *Getting Things Done: The Art of Stress-Free Productivity*. Penguin, 2002.

Chapter 4

1. Peter, Lawrence J. *The Peter Principle: Why Things Always Go Wrong*. Buccaneer Books, 1993.

2. www.eeoc.gov

3. www.archives.gov/education/lessons/civil-rights-act

4. Kaplan, Robert S. and Norton, David P. *The Balanced Scorecard: Translating Strategy into Action*. Harvard Business School Press, 1996.

5. http://en.wikipedia.org/wiki/SMART_(project_management)

6. Lencioni, Patrick. *Death by Meeting: A Leadership Fable...about Solving the Most Painful Problem in Business*. Jossey-Bass, 2004.

7. Greif, Michael. *The Visual Factory: Building Participation through Shared Information.* Productivity Press, 1991.

Chapter 5

1. McCoy, Marina. *Plato on the Rhetoric of Philosophers and Sophists.* Cambridge University Press, 2008, p. 77.

2. Coopersmith, Stanley. *The Antecedents of Self Esteem.* Consulting Psychologists Press, 1981.

3. Abraham, Richard. *Mr. Shmooze—The Art and Science of Selling through Relationships.* The Richard Abraham Company, 2002.

Chapter 6

1. Charan, Ram. *Sharpening Your Business Acumen.* Strategy+Business, Spring 2006, reprint No. 06106.

2. Yastrow, Steve. *We: The Ideal Customer Relationship.* Select Books, 2007.

3. Sicilano, Gene. *Finance for Non-Financial Managers (Briefcase Books Series).* McGraw Hill, 2003.

Index

360 survey, 8, 10, 17, 21, 43
Ableidinger, Bob, 35
Abraham, Richard, ix, 72, 97
Accountability, 41-60, 94
Alignment, 46-50
Allen, David, 35, 96
A-players, 49-53, 56
Arrogance, 10, 14-16, 44, 93
Articulation, 33
Assessment, talent, 27, 29, 42-43, 45
ATK, ix, 85
Authentic, 7, 9, 18-19

Babiasz, Jim, ix, 88
Balanced scorecards, 48, 57, 59, 88, 96
Bayles, Michael, 9, 49
Boards of directors, 1, 30, 54, 59, 86, 89
B-players, 51-53, 56
Brainstorm, 13, 20, 24-25, 56, 63, 80, 91
Brand, personal, 19, 83
Buddha, 11
Buffett, Warren, 84
Business acumen, 43, 79-91, 97

Cates, Jim, ix, 85
CEO, 1, 3, 5-6, 8-9, 16, 20-21, 23, 27-29, 31, 35, 38-40, 46, 55, 58, 67, 70, 74, 81, 87-90, 96
Charan, Ram, 79, 97
Churchill, Winston, 65
Civil Rights Act, 45, 96
Cleese, John, 67
Coaching, 12, 16-17, 19-20, 28, 34, 36, 42, 45-46, 53-54, 58, 62, 65-68, 80, 82
Collins, Jim, 2, 15, 95-96

Conceptual thinking, 3, 6, 27, 44, 90, 93
Confidence-modesty balance, 14-17, 19, 22, 27, 44, 57, 69, 93
Conflict, 11, 45, 50, 61-62, 64-65, 71, 73, 75-76, 82
Copernicus, 2, 95
C-players, 51-53, 56
Cross-training, 43
Customer, 8, 32, 42-43, 48, 51-53, 71, 73, 79-80, 82-84, 87, 90-91, 97

Dailey, Dave, ix, 87
Dannemiller, Kathy, 67
Death by Meeting, 49, 96
Decisiveness, 8-9, 18-19, 22, 32, 44, 67, 93
Defensible point of view, 19, 32-34, 40, 45-46, 81
Delegate, 36, 54-57
Detail versatility, 25-32, 44, 93
Developability, 45
Drucker, Peter, 46, 79
Dylan, Bob, 74

EEOC, 45, 96
Effective Edge, 34-35, 38, 96
Ego, 10, 14-17, 19, 22, 27, 51, 57, 69
Einstein, Albert, 4
Emotion, 1, 10, 12-13, 24-25, 34, 39, 44, 56, 61, 63, 69, 71-72, 74, 76, 93
Emotional intelligence, 44, 61, 93
Empowerment, 15, 24, 56
Engagement, 41, 51
Expectations, 1, 9, 23-40, 57, 70-72, 82-84, 91

Index

Facilitation, 51, 53
Fear, 16, 43, 46, 50-54, 57-59, 67-70, 72-74, 76
Feedback, 20-21, 43, 45-46, 52-53, 70
Financial acumen, 82-91, 97
Firefight, 11, 35
Fisher & Company, ix, 88
Frugality, 90

Graves, Gary, 32
Greenspan, Alan, 5, 95
Grip, Jeffrey, ix, 21, 95-96

Hemingway, Ernest, 12
Hiring, 41-46, 89

Impatience, 1, 12, 31, 33, 39, 44, 68, 93
Indecision, 18-19
Influence, 8, 12, 46, 59, 61-77
Integrity, 24, 44, 94
Interviewing, 1, 24, 43, 55, 65, 67

Jesus, 11
Job rotations, 4, 32, 43
Job-relatedness, 45

Lencioni, Patrick, 49, 58, 96
Life Success Seminars, 96
Listening, 2, 12, 15, 17, 28, 34, 44-45, 50, 55-57, 61, 65-69, 72, 77, 80, 82, 91, 94
LotusNotes®, 36-37

Master Chemical Corporation, ix, 46, 58
Matrix reporting, 51, 53
Meetings, 3, 30, 49, 55, 58, 66, 71, 73, 75, 80-81, 83-84, 89, 96
Mentor, 5, 8, 28, 31, 57, 76, 86, 89-90
Metrics, 8, 33, 39, 47-48, 50, 56-60, 84-85, 87-90
Minow, Nell, 27

Modesty, 14-17, 19, 22, 27, 44, 57, 69, 93

Negotiation, 47-48, 55, 65, 67, 76

Objectives (MBO) 17, 20, 24, 47-49, 59
Outlook®, 36-38
Overwhelm, 2, 16, 34-38, 51, 54

Performance review, 41, 43, 55, 65
Personal agendas, 3, 6, 16, 70-71
Persuasion, 55, 67
Peter Principle, 35, 42, 96
Powell, Colin, 18, 75
Priorities, 8, 20, 24-26, 29, 32, 35-40, 46-51, 57, 59, 62-64, 71, 80, 84, 88-90
Private equity, 1, 29
Procrastination, 12
Professional coach, 12, 17, 36, 68

Quanex Corporation, 9, 49

Randle, Christina, 35, 38, 96
Relationships, 44, 50, 61, 64-65, 69-74, 77, 81, 83-84, 97
Roles, 47, 53
Roosevelt, Eleanor, 76
Rotations, Job, 4, 32, 43

Self-esteem, 44, 57, 59, 61, 67-70, 72-73, 77, 93, 97
Shareholder, 8, 38, 82-84, 91
Sherwood, Steve, ix, 14, 95
Signature style, 8, 17, 19-22, 28-29, 50, 54, 74-75
SMART objective, 49
Social insight, 44, 93
Socrates, 66
Spath, Bob, ix, 90
SPX, ix, 50
Straight talk, 16, 39, 70, 73-74
Strategic, 6, 12, 18, 22, 29-32, 40, 43, 46-48, 50, 57, 59, 73, 80-82, 84, 89, 91

Surprises, 23, 38-40

Talent, 7, 8, 12, 18-19, 22, 27, 29-30, 33, 40-46, 49, 52, 54, 57-59, 64, 80
Talent assessment, 27, 29, 43, 45, 79
Technical thinker, 29
Tentative language, 33
Thin skin, 39, 69
Thoreau, Henry David, 2
Time management, 34-38
Tolle, Eckert, 14, 96
Trump, Donald, 22
Trust, 10, 15-16, 21, 64, 68, 70-74, 77

Uncertainty, 19, 38, 43, 51-54, 57, 59
Unleashing the Leader Within, 12
Unreasonableness, 16, 56-57

Values, 6, 11-14, 17, 20-22, 23-30, 33, 37, 39-40, 44-45, 57, 61-64, 77, 90, 94, 96
Verbosity, 30, 55, 65
Versatility, 21, 29-30, 43-45, 65, 93-94
Vocollect, 48

Welch, Jack, 10, 42, 73, 83
Wright, Joe, ix, 46, 58

Yastrow, Steve, ix, 83, 97
Young, Robertt, 34

Breinigsville, PA USA
20 July 2010
242157BV00002B/15/P